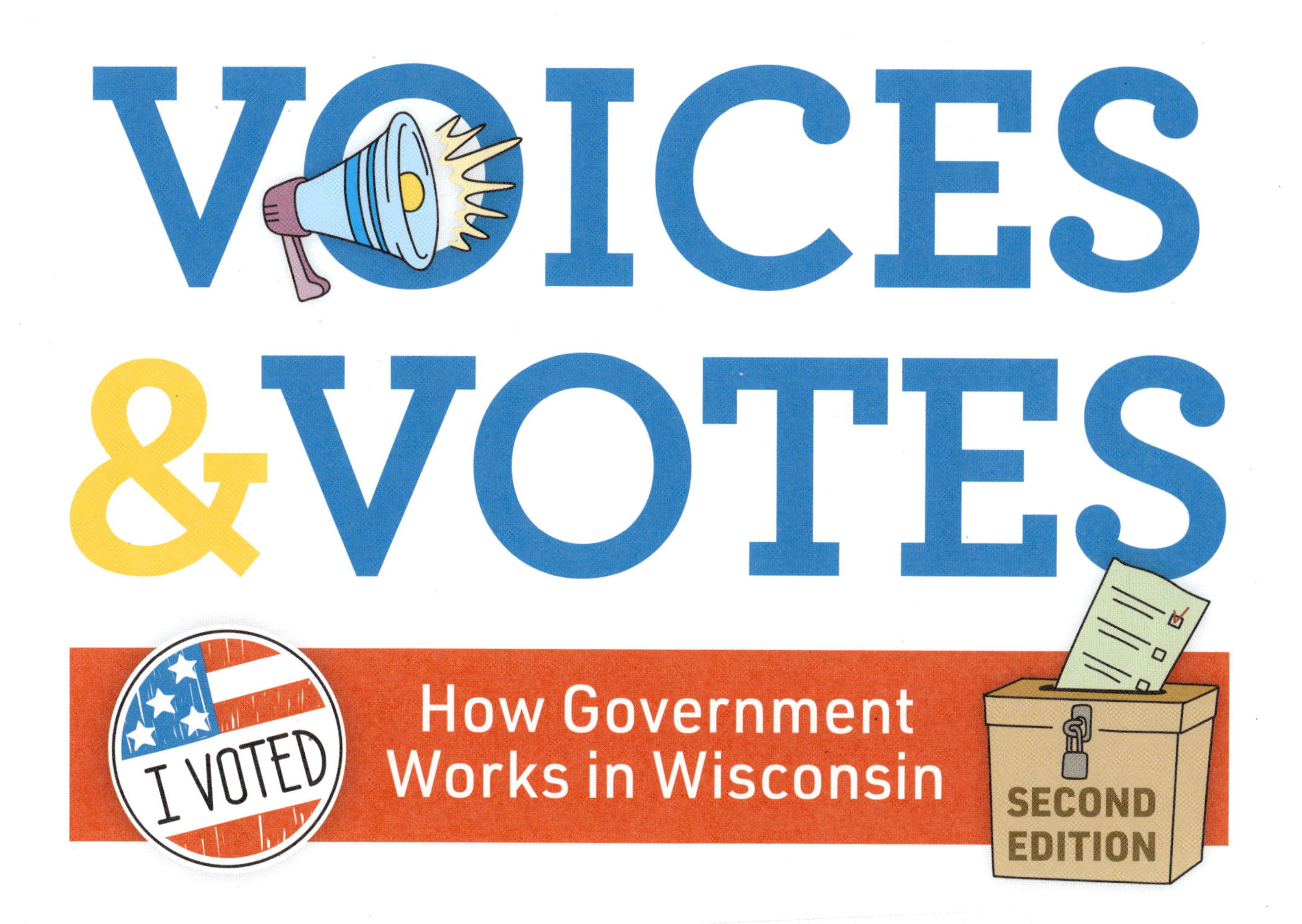

Wisconsin Historical Society Press

Published by the **Wisconsin Historical Society Press**
Publishers since 1855

The Wisconsin Historical Society helps people connect to the past by collecting, preserving, and sharing stories. Founded in 1846, the Society is one of the nation's finest historical institutions.

Join the Wisconsin Historical Society: **wisconsinhistory.org/membership**

Publication of this book was made possible in part by a grant from the D. C. Everest fellowship fund.

Front cover images: Student protesters, WHi image 115506. Shannon Holsey, John Hart/ *Wisconsin State Journal*. Girl with flag, WHi Image 109634. Mound protesters, WHi image 123836. Gaylord Nelson, WHi image 48016. Kids, iStock. Back cover image WHi Image ID 5157

Printed in Canada
Cover and interior pages designed by Shawn Biner

29 28 27 26 25 1 2 3 4 5

Library of Congress Cataloging-in-Publication Data
Names: Wisconsin Historical Society editor.
Title: Voices and votes : how government works in Wisconsin / Wisconsin Historical Society.
Other titles: Voices & votes
Description: Second edition. | Madison : Wisconsin Historical Society Press, [2025] | Revised edition of: Voices & votes. | Includes bibliographical references and index. | Audience: Ages 8–10 | Audience: Grades 4–6
Identifiers: LCCN 2024029732 (print) | LCCN 2024029733 (e-book) | ISBN 9781976600265 (paperback) | ISBN 9781976600272 (epub)
Subjects: LCSH: Wisconsin—Politics and government—1951—Textbooks.
Classification: LCC JK6016 .K37 2025 (print) | LCC JK6016 (e-book) | DDC 320.4775—dc23/eng/20240706
LC record available at https://lccn.loc.gov/2024029732
LC e-book record available at https://lccn.loc.gov/2024029733

♾ The paper used in this publication meets the minimum requirements of the American National Standard for Information Sciences—Permanence of Paper for Printed Library Materials, ANSI Z39.48-1992.

CONTENTS

INTRODUCTION

What do you think of when you hear the word *government*? The president of the United States? The governor of Wisconsin? These are government leaders. But our government is not just about its leaders. In a government, many people work together toward common goals. One goal is to keep people safe. Another goal is to create equal opportunities for everyone.

Governments meet their goals in two main ways. First, governments provide services. Some of these services are schools, parks, and fire departments. Second, governments make rules called laws. Speed limits on roads are laws. In Wisconsin, young people must go to school. That is another law. How do fire departments and speed limits keep people safe? How do schools and parks create equal opportunities?

This statue is called *Forward*. It stands outside Wisconsin's State Capitol. *Forward* is also Wisconsin's state motto. What does the word *forward* make you think about?

Our Government Is a Democracy

We in the United States have a kind of government known as a democracy (dih **mok** ruh see). Voting is one way that **citizens** (**sit** uh zuhnz) in a democracy make their voices heard. In the US, everyone born in the country is a citizen. Others can apply to

citizens: Members of a nation who have certain rights and responsibilities

elections: The process of voting to choose government leaders

govern: To rule, lead, or be in charge of a group of people

responsibilities: Duties or jobs

become US citizens. Today, US citizens over the age of 18 are allowed to vote. In some cities, people as young as 16 can vote in local **elections** (i **lek** shuhnz).

In our democracy, voters choose government leaders. Those leaders represent (rep pri **zent**) us in government. That means they speak and act for all of us. They are supposed to make decisions based on the needs and wants of all the people they represent. In this way, the people of our country **govern** (**guh** vurn) themselves. Because we live in a democracy, the government is really us.

In our democracy, all people have rights and **responsibilities** (ri spon suh **bil** uh teez). Our democracy gives people the *right* to govern themselves. But people have the *responsibility* to use that right by voting. Our democracy gives people the *right* to have a say in the laws that are made. But people have the *responsibility* to follow those laws.

Everyone Can Work for Change

In a democracy, everyone has the right to change their lives for the better. Voting is an important way to do this. But there are other ways to make change. Some people choose to speak up and take action. It's not always easy. Not everyone who tries to make change is successful. But if nobody ever tried, then nothing would ever change!

Every chapter in this book starts with a story from Wisconsin's past. The stories tell about people who wanted to make change. They wanted a better future. They got involved with their government to make it happen.

Change happens today, too. People are working right now for change across Wisconsin. They're getting involved with their communities and governments. They're paying attention. They're speaking up. They're taking action.

Young people like you cannot yet vote. You cannot yet become government leaders. But you don't have to wait to get involved. Each chapter in this book ends with a story about young people in Wisconsin who took action. They shared their voices. They worked for change. Maybe these stories will inspire you to get involved, too. You can make a difference. You can help make Wisconsin's democracy work better for all who live here.

This photo was taken in 1962 in Madison. These high school students did not want their school to close. They chose to protest. Protesting is a way to make change. But it is not the only way. You'll learn about others as you read this book.

CHAPTER 1

The Levels of Our Government

discrimination: Treating some people worse than others without a fair reason

office: A job in government

Gaylord Nelson was born in Clear Lake, Wisconsin, in 1916. From an early age, Nelson cared about the environment. At age 12, he stood in front of the Clear Lake city council. He asked them to plant trees in the city. As Nelson grew older, he became even more concerned about the environment. He wanted everyone to have clean air, water, and land. Nelson also saw that people of color often faced discrimination (dis krim uh **nay** shun). He wanted all people to be treated fairly. But how could he get what he wanted? He decided to run for government office (**ah** fis).

Senator Gaylord Nelson speaks on the first Earth Day in 1970.

When he was 32 years old, Nelson was elected as a state **senator** (**sen** uh tur). Nelson helped pass laws to protect the rights of people of color. Later he became Wisconsin's governor. As governor, he created laws to protect the environment from polluters. Still, he wanted to do more. Nelson ran for the office of US senator and won. As a US senator, he kept fighting for people of color to be treated fairly. He also kept working to preserve the environment. Today, Nelson is best known as the creator of Earth Day. On Earth Day, people across the country show support for the environment.

Nelson got involved with all three levels of US government: **federal** (**fed** ur uhl), state, and local. In this chapter, you'll learn more about these levels of government. You'll also learn about Tribal government. There are many Native nations in the US, and they have their own citizens and governments.

senator: A person elected to serve in a part of government called the senate

federal: A type of government where its smaller sections (such as states) are united under one central government but keep certain powers

Questions to Think About

- **What's the difference between state government and federal government?**
- **Why are there three levels of US government?**
- **What does each level of US government do?**
- **What kind of governments do Native nations have?**

Federal Government

In the United States, all 50 states are united under the federal government. Washington, DC, is our nation's capital city. That is where our federal government is based.

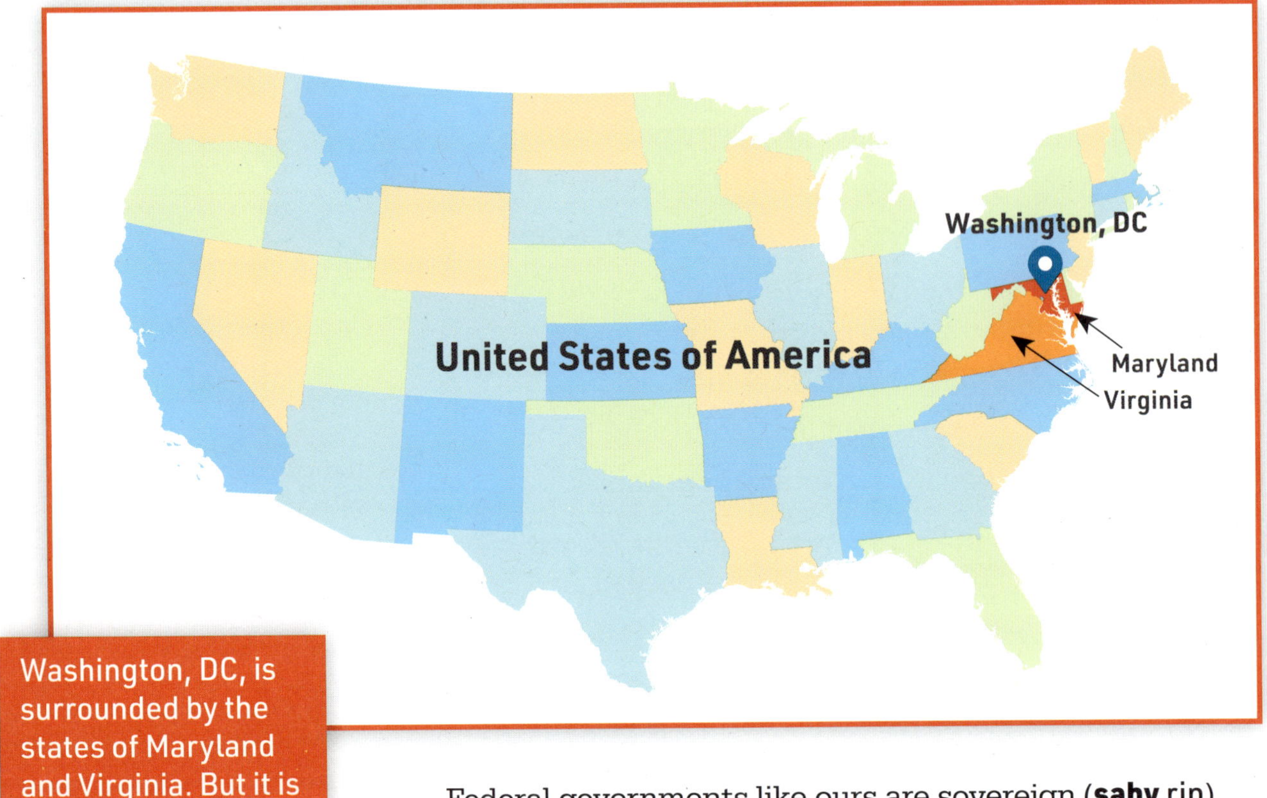

Washington, DC, is surrounded by the states of Maryland and Virginia. But it is not part of any state.

Federal governments like ours are sovereign (**sahv** rin). This means that our nation has the right to govern itself. No other nation has a say over the decisions a sovereign government makes.

Our federal government has three branches:

1. Executive (eg **zek** yoo tiv)
2. Legislative (**lej** uh slay tiv)
3. Judicial (joo **dish** uhl)

enforce: To make sure that a rule or law is obeyed

The executive branch is the part of government that **enforces** (in **fors** iz) laws. The leader of the executive branch is the president. The president also leads the federal government.

The legislative branch is also called the legislature (**lej** uh slay chur). The legislature is the part of government that makes laws. The people who make up the federal legislative branch come from every state. Legislators (**lej** uh slay turz) are people who are elected to the legislature.

In the federal government, legislators make up the US Congress (**kon** gris). Congress is split into two law-making groups, or houses. One is called the Senate (**sen** uht). In the Senate, states are represented equally. Every state has two senators. The other house is called the House of Representatives (rep pri **zen** tuh tivz). States have different numbers of representatives. Those numbers are based on how many people live in a state.

The third branch of the federal government is the judicial branch. It solves disagreements about what federal laws mean. The US Supreme (suh **preem**) Court is the head of the federal judicial branch.

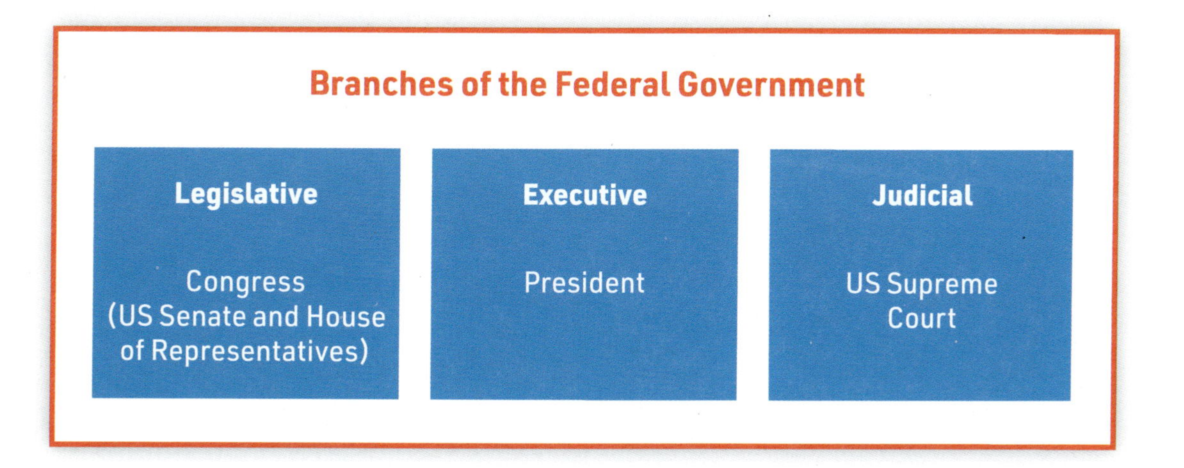

People in every state must obey federal laws. Federal laws are called acts. For example, there is a federal law called the Americans with Disabilities Act. It protects people with disabilities from discrimination no matter where they live in the US.

State and Local Government

In the US, each state also has its own government. State governments also have three branches: executive, legislative, and judicial. The head of the state's executive branch is the governor. The Wisconsin state government makes and enforces laws within the state's borders. Everyone who lives in or visits Wisconsin must follow those laws. But Wisconsin's government cannot make laws for other states. Each state's government is **independent** of the others.

independent: Not controlled or ruled by another

Wisconsin also has many smaller local governments. Each county, city, village, and town in Wisconsin has its own local government. Local governments make laws and provide services for their own communities. A city might have a law about when people can be in public parks. A county might run a snowplow service to clear the county roads in winter.

You'll learn more about what state and local governments do later in this book.

Why Do We Have Three Levels of US Government?

You might wonder why we can't have just one level of US government. Wouldn't that be easier? But all three levels of government are needed. Each level has different

The people in this 2011 photo represent three levels of US government. At left is Green Bay mayor Jim Schmitt (local). In the middle is Wisconsin governor Scott Walker (state). At right is US president Barack Obama (federal).

responsibilities. It is better to make some decisions at the local level. The US president cannot decide the speed limit for every street in the country! What if the governor had to run one snowplow service for the whole state?

The federal government deals with issues that affect the whole country. For example, it makes our nation's money. Everyone in the US uses dollars and cents. Imagine how confusing it would be if every state had a different kind of money!

State governments deal with issues that affect the whole state. Wisconsin's state government manages state highways. It protects land, water, and wildlife across the state. It also runs a statewide system of universities.

Local governments have their own responsibilities. The state cannot plow everyone's streets in winter. Instead, the county or city does it. Many cities have their own police and fire departments.

Having three levels of US government allows people to do what is best for their communities. State and local governments are supposed to make decisions based on their communities' needs and wants. People in Wisconsin have different needs and wants than people in California. And people in Milwaukee have different needs and wants than people in Superior.

Why might the people who live in the places shown here have different wants and needs? What might some of those wants and needs be?

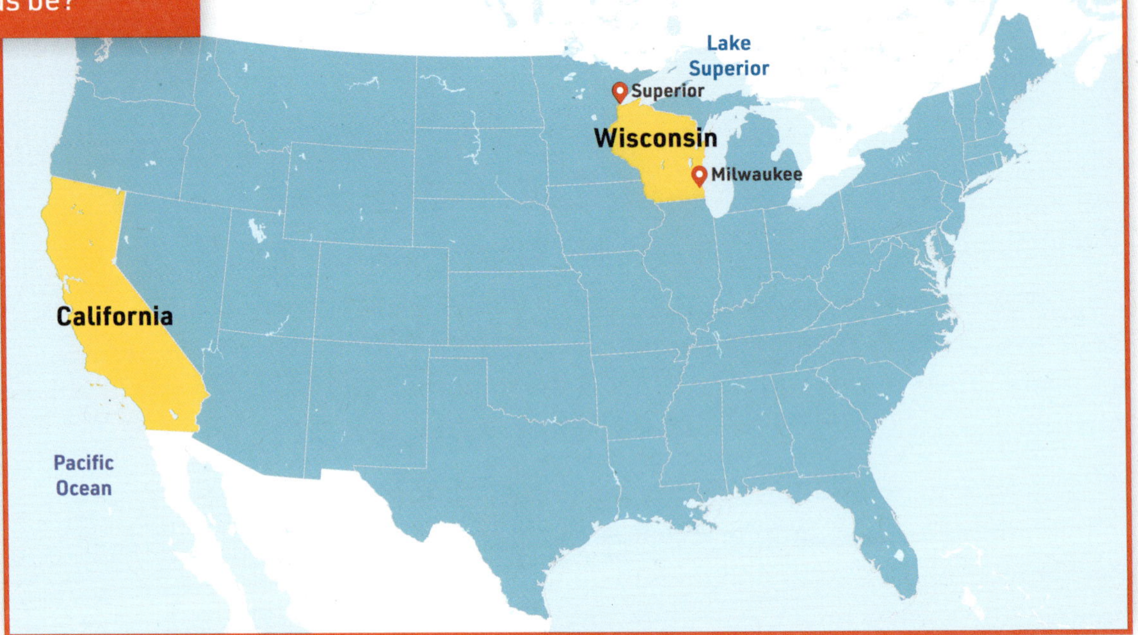

Tribal Governments

Native nations are nations within the US. Just like the federal government, Native nations are sovereign. They have a right to govern themselves. Citizens of Native nations are also citizens of the United States.

Each Native nation has its own Tribal government. Tribal citizens elect their government leaders. Tribal government leaders make and enforce their nation's laws. Tribal leaders make decisions that affect their citizens as well as non-Native people. Tribal governments work with the US government. They have "government-to-government" relationships with federal and state governments.

Look at the diagram. Tribal government appears at the top. It is right next to the federal government. In many ways, Tribal governments are independent of state and federal government. But Tribal governments must also follow some state and federal laws. Take another look at the diagram. See the arrows? They point from Tribal government to federal and state government. The three work together toward common goals.

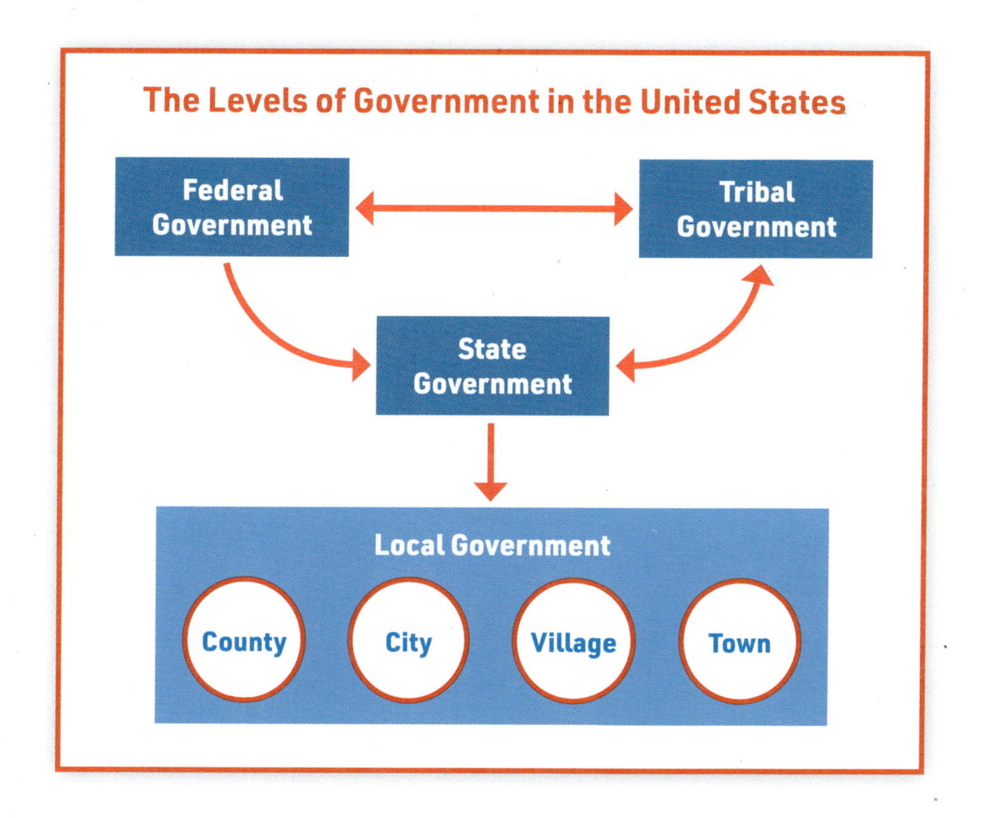

Today, there are 12 Native nations in Wisconsin. They are:

- Bad River Band of Lake Superior Chippewa
- Brothertown Nation
- Forest County Potawatomi (**pah** tuh **wah** tuh mee)
- Ho-Chunk Nation
- Lac Courte Oreilles (lah **coo** dor **ay**) Band of Lake Superior Chippewa
- Lac du Flambeau (**lahk** du flahm **boh**) Band of Lake Superior Chippewa
- Menominee (muh **nah** muh nee) Indian Tribe of Wisconsin
- Oneida Nation
- Red Cliff Band of Lake Superior Chippewa
- Sokaogon (suh **kah** gin) Chippewa Community (Mole Lake Band)
- St. Croix (saynt croy) Chippewa Indians of Wisconsin
- Stockbridge-Munsee Community Band of Mohican Indians

Every year, the leader of a Wisconsin Native nation gives a statewide speech. It is called the State of the Tribes Address. In 2022, Shannon Holsey (pictured here) gave the speech. She was president of the Stockbridge-Munsee at the time.

Of the 12 Native nations in Wisconsin, 11 are recognized by the federal government. The Brothertown Nation is not. That means the Brothertown Nation does not have a "government-to-government" relationship with US federal and state governments.

Two hundred years ago, the land that is now called Wisconsin was home to several Native nations. During the 1800s, non-Native people began to move to this region. Some came straight from Europe. Others had come from Europe years before and settled in other parts of the US. Native peoples had lived on this land for thousands of years. But the US government wanted their lands for white settlers. The US government forced the Native nations to

Compare the lands that belonged to Wisconsin Native nations in 1825 (left) and today (right). What do you notice?

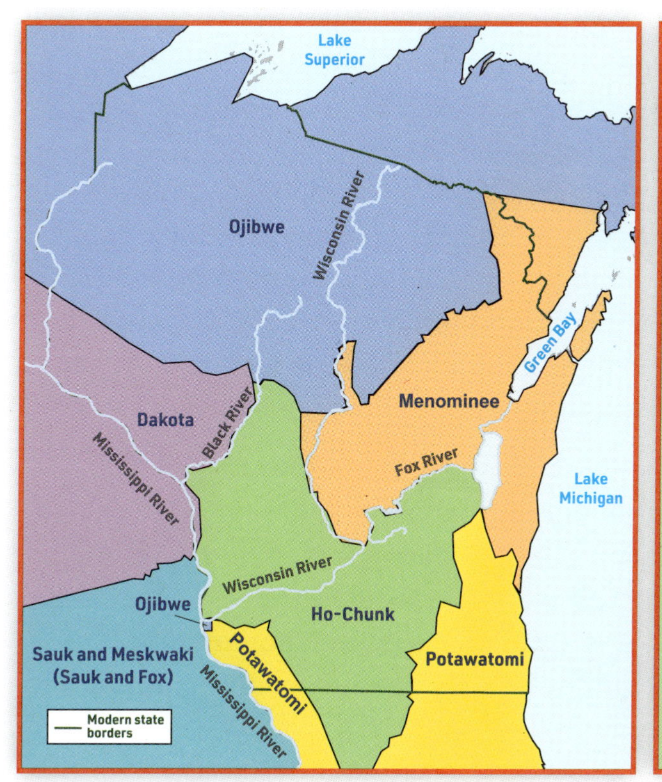

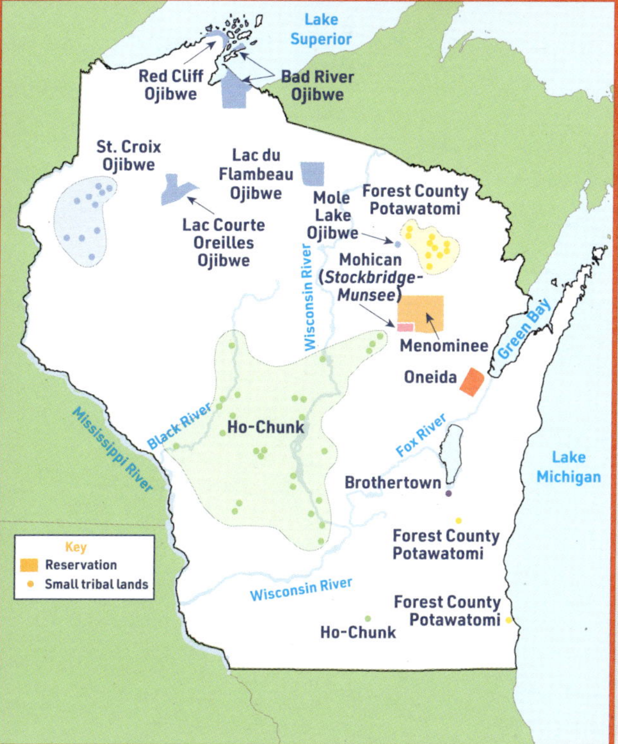

sign treaties (**tree** teez) with them. A treaty is an agreement between sovereign nations. Treaties describe certain rights and rules. But they are not always fair.

As part of these treaties, Native nations were forced to cede (seed), or give up, most of their land. The federal government took ownership of this land. Then the government sold the land to new, non-Native settlers. The US government forced most Native nations to move to **reservations** (rez ur **vay** shuhnz). Sometimes, the reservation was on the nation's original land. Other times, the reservation was far from their homeland.

reservations: Areas in the US set aside by treaty for Native nations after those nations ceded their original lands

The People's Voice

Voting gives people a voice in our democracy. How? People's voices are heard when they vote for the leaders they want to represent them. People vote for leaders at all three levels of US government: federal, state, and local. Tribal citizens vote for their government leaders, too. Government leaders try to listen to the people they represent. How else would they know what those people need and want? Still, sometimes people don't like the decisions their government leaders make. Then, they can vote for someone else in the next election.

Voting is not the only way that people can have a voice in their government. People can write to their government leaders. They can talk to those leaders in person. They can let leaders know about problems in their communities. They can help their government leaders make decisions and provide services.

Government leaders don't represent only people who can vote. They represent young people like you, too. Did you know that you can share your opinions with your government leaders? A way to do that is by writing a letter. In 2021, that is what Marcia Gardner's fourth-grade class did.

Ms. Gardner teaches at Southern Bluffs Elementary School in La Crosse. In 2021, the federal government sent money to her school so students could have free breakfast. Many adults had lost work during the COVID-19 **pandemic** (pan **de** mik) starting in 2020. Lots of families had less money than usual. Free school breakfasts were a big help during that hard time. But then Ms. Gardner found out that free breakfasts at her school might come to an end.

pandemic: When many people in a country or the world get the same disease at the same time

Ms. Gardner told her class that they might not have free breakfast anymore. Her students were worried. They had to do something about it! Ms. Gardner suggested they write letters to their members of Congress. Members of Congress would decide whether to keep paying for students' breakfasts. Those members should know what the students thought.

First, Ms. Gardner's fourth graders did research. They went online. They had a guest speaker visit their class. They gathered facts about why breakfast is important for young people. Those facts helped the students back up their opinions with **evidence** (**ev** uh dents). Next, the students learned how to write a formal letter. They helped improve their classmates' work. Then, they rewrote their letters in

evidence: Information and facts that help prove something or make you believe something is true

"Breakfast is just as important as books and materials because kids can't really pay attention if they are hungry."

"Free breakfast is easier for families. Parents don't have to worry about what to make and it is free quality food with a lot of variety."

– From the letters Ms. Gardner's students wrote

their best handwriting. Ms. Gardner mailed the letters to the legislators. Her students received letters back from all of them!

Still, Congress voted to stop sending money for free school breakfasts. Ms. Gardner's students didn't get what they wanted. But they knew their voices had been heard. Why do you think that's important?

Brad Lussier teaches seventh-grade geography at DeForest Area Middle School. His students write to government officials every year. They share their voice on many different issues. During the COVID-19 pandemic, local government leaders had to decide whether schools would stay open. This issue affected Mr. Lussier's students in a big way! The students wrote letters to their local leaders. They shared their opinions about going back to school. They made sure their voices were heard.

When Mr. Lussier's students write letters to government leaders, they follow these steps:

- First, choose an issue that matters to you.
- Next, ask yourself which side you are on and why.
- Research the issue to gather facts and evidence. Try to understand all sides of the issue.
- Think about what you have learned. Ask yourself if your opinion has changed or stayed the same.
- Choose whom you will write to.
    - Is it a local issue? Write to your mayor or city council person.

  - Is it a state issue? Write to your state legislator or governor.
  - Is it a federal issue? Write to your members of Congress or the president. Yes, you can write a letter to the president of the United States!
  - Is it a Tribal issue? Write to Tribal leadership.
- When you write your letter, remember:
  - It's important to support your opinion with evidence.
  - It's okay to disagree with the person you're writing to as long as you are respectful.
- Have someone else read your letter. Ask them to give you suggestions on how to make it better.
- Find the right email or office address for the person you're writing to. Most government officials have websites where you can find this information.
- Finally, send the letter!

You can follow the same steps to write to your government leaders. To find out who your state or federal legislators are, go to **legis.wisconsin.gov** (state) or **congress.gov/members/find-your-member** (federal). To find out who Tribal leaders are, visit each nation's website. You can find a list of them all at **dpi.wi.gov/amind/tribalnationswi**. You can also find addresses on those sites. Writing a letter does not mean that you will get what you want. But it is a great way to share your voice.

CHAPTER 2

The Wisconsin Constitution

All democracies have constitutions (kon stuh **too** shuhnz). What is a constitution? It is a list of the people's rights and responsibilities. It describes how the government will work.

You have probably heard of the US Constitution. But did you know that every state has its own constitution? Or that every Native nation in Wisconsin has its own constitution? In this chapter, you'll learn more about what constitutions do. You'll learn how Wisconsin created its first constitution. You'll also learn how constitutions can change. Of course, they don't change all on their own. First,

In 1960, a woman from Germany and a woman from Japan study a booklet about the US Constitution. They were studying to become US citizens.

someone must suggest a change. Then legislators and voters decide whether they agree.

In 1982, the Wisconsin Constitution was 134 years old. Some of its language sounded old-fashioned. The Constitution said, "All men are born equally free and independent." Those words were written in 1848. The word *men* was not meant to leave out women. Back then, people used words like *men* and *mankind* to mean all people. By the 1980s, that had changed. Words like *people* and *humankind* had become more common.

Wisconsin legislators wanted to change the state constitution's language. By law, Wisconsin's voters had to approve the change. In the November 1982 election, voters were asked if they wanted to change the language. The *yes* votes won, and the change was made. Today, the Wisconsin Constitution says, "All people are born equally free and independent."

Questions to Think About

- **What does a constitution do?**
- **What rights and responsibilities does a constitution mention?**
- **Why was Wisconsin's first constitution voted down?**
- **Why might a constitution need to change?**

Constitutions Define Basic Rights and Responsibilities

Do you know how the US Constitution begins? "We the people of the United States." The first words of the Wisconsin Constitution are "We, the people of Wisconsin." The Menominee constitution begins "We, the members of the Menominee Indian Tribe of Wisconsin." Why do constitutions begin this way?

Our constitutions explain people's rights and responsibilities. Everyone has a responsibility to follow their city, state, and country's rules. But along with this responsibility come many important rights. A constitution defines what those rights are. The US Constitution has a Bill of Rights. This is a list of freedoms the authors thought were the most important. The Wisconsin Constitution has something similar. It is called a Declaration of Rights. The Menominee Nation's constitution lists the rights of Tribal citizens.

Both the US and Wisconsin Constitutions protect free speech. This gives every person the right to express their ideas and opinions. Constitutions protect this right by promising that governments cannot punish people for expressing their ideas. People in the US and Wisconsin have freedom of speech, religion, and the press. This means that all people can speak freely on any subject. They can worship in any way they want. They can publish anything they want. It is against the law to take away these rights.

It is very important to protect people's right to do certain things. But it is equally important to make sure that certain things cannot be done to people. The writers of the US and Wisconsin Constitutions didn't want their governments to

PREAMBLE

We, the people of Wisconsin, grateful to Almighty God for our freedom, in order to secure its blessings, form a more perfect government, insure domestic tranquility and promote the general welfare, do establish this constitution.

ARTICLE I.
DECLARATION OF RIGHTS

Equality; inherent rights. SECTION 1. [*As amended Nov. 1982 and April 1986*] All people are born equally free and independent, and have certain inherent rights; among these are life, liberty and the pursuit of happiness; to secure these rights, governments are instituted, deriving their just powers from the consent of the governed. [*1979 J.R. 36, 1981 J.R. 29, vote Nov. 1982; 1983 J.R. 40, 1985 J.R. 21, vote April 1986*]

Slavery prohibited. SECTION 2. There shall be neither slavery, nor involuntary servitude in this state, otherwise than for the punishment of crime, whereof the party shall have been duly convicted.

Free speech; libel. SECTION 3. Every person may freely speak, write and publish his sentiments on all subjects, being responsible for the abuse of that right, and no laws shall be passed to restrain or abridge the liberty of speech or of the press. In all criminal prosecutions or indictments for libel, the truth may be given in evidence, and if it shall appear to the jury that the matter charged as libelous be true, and was published with good motives and for justifiable ends, the party shall be acquitted; and the jury shall have the right to determine the law and the fact.

become too powerful. So they listed things that government officials can never do. Think of these two sets of rights as "freedoms to" and "freedoms from." Here are examples of rights from the US and Wisconsin Constitutions. Which are "freedoms to"? Which are "freedoms from"?

- The government cannot put you in jail for no reason.
- You can gather with others to protest against a government decision.
- The government cannot search your private property without permission.
- If you're accused of a crime, you have the right to a trial (**trI** uhl) by jury (**jur** ee).
- Adult citizens have the right to run for government office.

The first three rights in the Wisconsin Constitution have to do with equality, forbidding slavery, and allowing free speech. Why do you think these three come first?

trial: The hearing and judgment of a case in court

jury: A group of adult citizens who decide the result of a trial

These people gathered at the Wisconsin State Capitol in 2016. They were using their free speech rights to protest a law that would reduce protections for Native burial mounds.

With basic rights come some basic responsibilities. Members of a democracy have the responsibility to:

- Obey laws
- Help make laws by voting for legislators
- Try to change laws that they believe are unjust
- Choose the best people to be government leaders
- Pay attention to how well government leaders do their jobs
- Pay taxes (**taks** iz), or money that makes government services, such as parks and fire departments, possible

Can you think of other responsibilities that people have in a democracy?

Constitutions Describe Government

Constitutions also explain how a government will work. For example, the US Constitution created the office of the

US president, the US Congress, and the US Supreme Court. The US constitution also explains:

- How the president is elected
- How states choose members of Congress
- How the US Supreme Court works

The Wisconsin Constitution describes how state government will work. For example, it explains:

- How to make state laws
- How the people select state legislators
- How state government enforces laws, collects taxes, and provides services

Tribal constitutions describe how Tribal governments will work. For example, they explain:

- The powers of the Tribal legislature
- How many members the Tribal legislature should have
- How Tribal legislators are elected

The Story of Wisconsin's First Constitution

Wisconsin's first constitution was approved in 1848. It was not an easy process. Before it became a state, Wisconsin was a **territory** (**tair** uh tor ee). People living in a territory do not have the same rights as those who live in a state.

territory: A piece of land that belongs to the US but is not a state

Before 1836, the land in what we now call Wisconsin belonged to Native nations. In 1836, the US Congress created the Wisconsin Territory. The federal government made the Native nations sign treaties. Those treaties forced Native nations to cede most of the land. Some Native peoples were forced to move out of the state. Others were

Native nations were forced to sign treaties with the US government. With these treaties, they ceded much of their land. This painting shows the treaty making at Prairie du Chien in 1825.

appointed: Chose a person for a particular job or duty

forced to live on reservations. By 1848, almost all the land in the Wisconsin Territory was owned by the federal government or by white settlers. The settlers were people who came to Wisconsin from other parts of the US or Europe. They created the Wisconsin Territory's government. Native people were not allowed to participate in that government. How do you think this affected Native people?

The US president in 1836 was Andrew Jackson. He **appointed** (uh **poin** tid) Henry Dodge as the Wisconsin Territory's first governor. The people of the Wisconsin Territory elected a small legislature. Still, the people did not have a say in federal government.

By April 1846, Wisconsin had been a US territory for ten years. While many Native peoples were being forced out, more European and American settlers had moved into the Wisconsin Territory. It was time to become a state. In a state, citizens would have a greater voice in government. They would be able to:

- Elect their own governor
- Make and enforce laws for themselves

- Send more representatives and two senators to Congress
- Help elect a president
- Raise their own money through taxes
- Decide how to spend their own tax money

A territory had to write a constitution before it could become a state. That is exactly what the people of Wisconsin did next.

A Failure Before Success

In the fall of 1846, the Wisconsin Territory's voters elected 124 **delegates** (**de** li guhts) to form a **convention** (kuhn **ven** shuhn). The convention met in Madison to write a constitution. But getting voters to approve that constitution was difficult. Wisconsin had to have two votes before the constitution was approved.

delegates: People selected to represent other people at a meeting

convention: A large gathering of people who share similar interests

For months, the delegates discussed how the state government should work. They discussed which rights and responsibilities people should have. They decided on some parts of the constitution quickly. For example, delegates agreed to make the office of the governor. This was very similar to governors' offices in other states.

Some questions were harder to resolve. Should court judges be elected by the people? Or should the governor appoint them? In the US Constitution, the president appoints federal judges. Many states followed this example. Other states let the people choose judges through elections. Many Wisconsin delegates thought that electing judges was more democratic. There was a lot of **debate** (di **bayt**) about the question. Finally, the delegates decided that the people of Wisconsin should elect their judges.

debate: A discussion between sides with different points of view

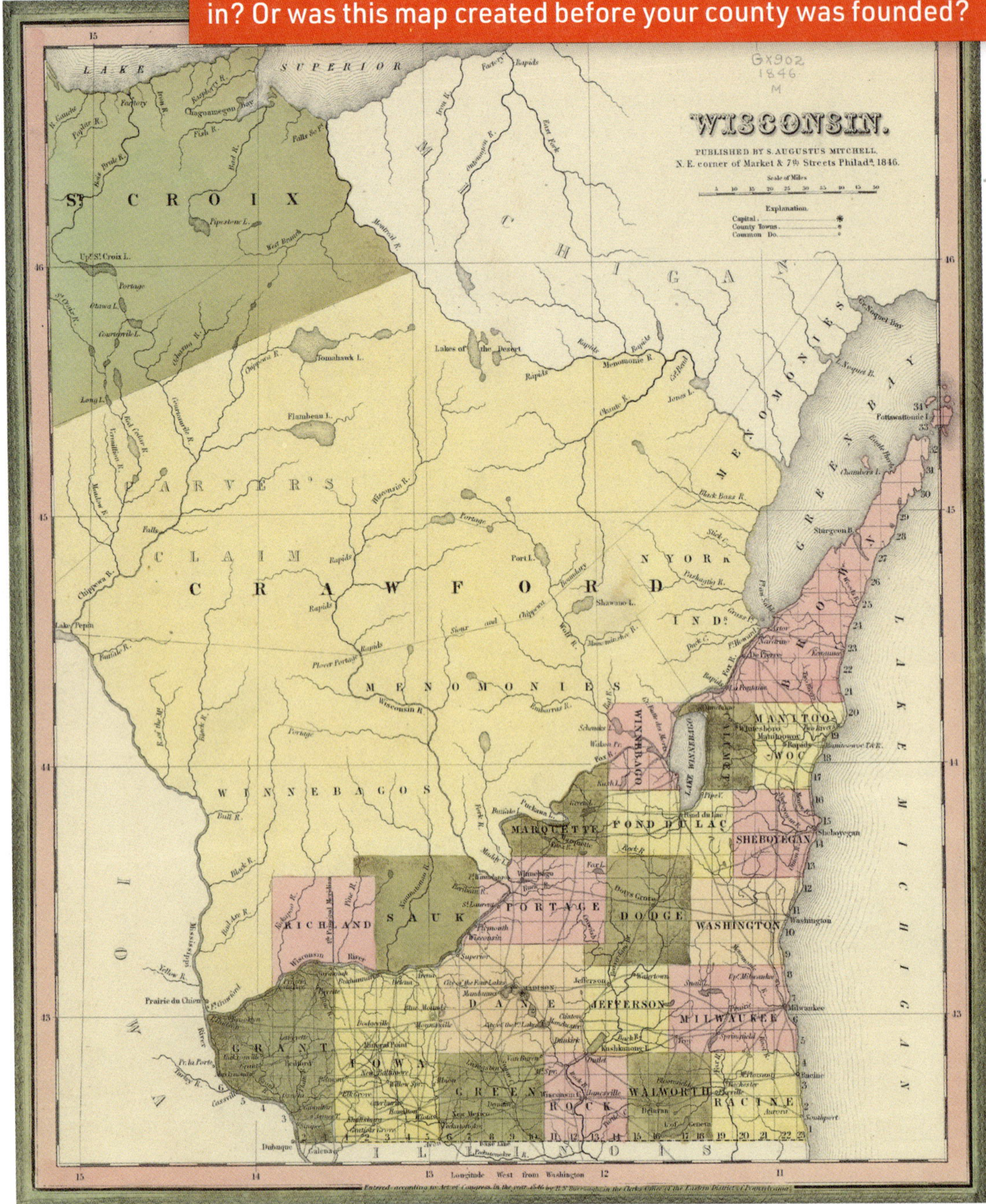

This map of the Wisconsin Territory was drawn in 1846. Then, there were fewer counties and towns than Wisconsin has today. Crawford County took up most of the state. Can you find the county you live in? Or was this map created before your county was founded?

The delegates disagreed about other parts of the constitution. Many of them were not happy with the convention's decisions. For example, the constitution gave married women the right to own property. A woman's husband did not have to own that property, too. Many delegates were against this. They worked to defeat the constitution when the people of Wisconsin voted on it. In the end, more Wisconsin citizens voted against it than for it. What would happen next?

The Wisconsin state flag includes the year that Wisconsin became a state: 1848.

In the fall of 1847, Governor Henry Dodge called a special meeting of the legislature. The legislature passed a law calling for a new convention. This convention would meet on December 15. It would have 69 delegates instead of 124. The smaller number of delegates made the convention easier to manage. Those delegates made changes to the constitution of 1846.

In March 1848, the people of Wisconsin voted on the constitution again. This time, 75 percent of the voters approved it. On May 29, 1848, Wisconsin became a state. It also became part of the US federal government.

Constitutions Can Change

The US and Wisconsin Constitutions can be changed. So can Native nations' constitutions. Changes to a constitution are called amendments (uh **mend** muhntz). The Wisconsin Constitution's writers made it hard to approve amendments. Why? They did not want a small group of people to be able to make changes to please only themselves. That is why amending the state constitution is a long process. It involves legislators and the voters. The legislature must

Patrick Lucey (center) celebrates winning the race for governor in 1970. Lucey was the first Wisconsin governor to serve a four-year term.

term: The period of time that elected officials can serve before they must run for office again

approve an amendment twice. Then the people vote for or against the amendment.

Between 1848 and 2020, the people in Wisconsin approved 146 changes to the state constitution. For example, Wisconsin voters passed an amendment in 1967 that gave governors four-year **terms**. Before that, governors were elected to two-year terms. As time goes on, people's needs and wants change. The Wisconsin Constitution could be amended again in the future.

GETTING INVOLVED

The US and Wisconsin Constitutions give people the right to free speech. This right applies to young people, too.

Some young people in Madison use their right to free speech to help their community. They publish articles in a newspaper called the *Simpson Street Free Press*. Students in third grade through high school can write for the newspaper. Students choose topics that interest them. They interview experts. They do research. Then they write articles. Finally, they revise their work to make it the best it can be.

Students have written about local issues that affect them. Some have written about the number of students who need more help learning to read. Those writers researched how reading is taught in Madison schools. They learned about other ways to teach reading. In their articles, they argued that schools in Madison should change the way they teach reading. People at the schools read their articles. So did other people in the community. Because of their articles, students even got to interview their school superintendent. They asked questions to find out how he would fix the problem.

The *Simpson Street Free Press* can be found all over Madison. It is also online. Anyone can learn from the articles that the students write.

"As a Madison high school student, I see it every day. It causes me pause to see the numbing number of local children who right now need the benefit of new and better approaches to literacy."

– From a *Simpson Street Free Press* article

CHAPTER 3

Who Are the Voters in Wisconsin?

In a democracy, the people rule themselves by electing those they want to govern them. A vote is a voice in a democracy. But who can vote in elections? Today in Wisconsin, all US citizens over age 18 can vote. But that wasn't always true. In the past, some citizens were denied the right to vote in the state. Some took steps to win that right.

Ezekiel (i **zee** kee uhl) Gillespie was born in Tennessee in 1818. He was the son of an enslaved woman. He was enslaved, too. In 1851, Gillespie purchased his freedom and moved to Milwaukee. He owned a grocery store in the city. He became a respected leader in Milwaukee's Black

An undated photo of Ezekiel Gillespie

community. Gillespie was a free man. He was a business owner and a responsible citizen. But because of the color of his skin, he wasn't allowed to vote. He had no say in his government.

Gillespie knew that was wrong. He wanted to change the law. So during an 1865 election, Gillespie filled out a **ballot** (**ba** luht). He tried to turn it in. But the election workers refused to accept it.

Gillespie was taking a big risk by trying to vote. But to him, it was worth the risk. His actions might help change the law. If Black people had a voice in their government, their lives could change for the better. Did Gillespie's actions lead to change? You'll find out later in this chapter. You'll also learn about two other groups who were denied the right to vote in Wisconsin: women and Native people.

ballot: A secret way of voting, such as on a machine or on a slip of paper

Questions to Think About

- **Why is the right to vote so important?**
- **Why have some people been denied the right to vote in the US?**
- **Why were Native people denied the right to vote for so long?**
- **How have our ideas changed about who should be able to vote?**

Who Could Vote in Wisconsin in 1848?

People's rights and responsibilities were written into the Wisconsin Constitution in 1848. But that constitution also denied some people the right to vote. When it was first written, the constitution said that men could vote, but not women. However, Black men could not vote. Women and Black men had no voice in making the laws. But they still had to obey all those laws.

The 1848 state constitution allowed only some Native men to vote. This included Native men that Congress had declared to be US citizens. At that time, most Native men in Wisconsin were not US citizens. If Native people wanted to become US citizens, they had to reject citizenship in their Native nation. Native people had to give up a lot for the right to vote in federal and state elections.

The people in this photo from 1954 had recently become US citizens. They are registering to vote in Wisconsin.

The 1848 Wisconsin constitution also said that only US citizens could vote. People born in the US are called natural-born citizens. People born in another country can apply to become citizens.

The Wisconsin legislature could pass a law that would give a group of people the right to vote. But voters would also have to support such a change. As you'll see, those voters often refused.

Black Wisconsinites Fight for the Vote

In 1846, many Black people were still enslaved in the southern United States. Some free Black people lived in the northern states, including Wisconsin. But they were seldom allowed to vote.

The first time Wisconsin voters were asked to vote on the state's constitution, they were also asked another question. They were asked if Black men should be able to vote in Wisconsin. As many as 14,119 people voted *yes*. But 20,333 people voted *no*. The *no* votes won. Black men still could not vote in the state.

People who thought Black men should have the right to vote tried again. In 1849, the legislature suggested a law to give Black men the right to vote. This time, very few people voted on the law. Only about 17 out of every 100 voters voted. Out of the people who did vote, most were in favor of giving Black men the right to vote. The results were 5,265 in favor and 4,075 against. It seemed as if Black men would win the vote. But government officials ruled that

A photo of the Henderson family taken around 1885. Notley Henderson (bottom right) first came to Madison in the 1860s. He and his wife, Martha (bottom center), married in the 1880s. Their family continued to live in Madison.

the election failed. Why? Because so few people had voted. Once again, Black men in Wisconsin were denied the right to vote.

Black people continued to fight for the right to vote. A large group met in Milwaukee in 1855. They demanded that the legislature try again. The legislature heard their demand. They put the question to the voters two more times, in 1857 and in 1865. Both times, the people denied Black men the right to vote.

sued: Started a legal case against someone in a court of law

Then an amazing thing happened. In the 1865 election, Ezekiel Gillespie filled out a ballot. When his ballot was refused, Gillespie **sued** (**sood**) the election officials. He insisted that he should have the right to vote.

Gillespie's case went before the Wisconsin Supreme Court in 1866. The three justices considered the matter. They decided that the vote of 1849 should not have failed. True, only 17 out of every 100 voters had voted. But most of those people voted in favor of allowing Black men to vote. The court ruled that Black men should have been able to vote in Wisconsin since 1849. Ezekiel Gillespie had helped change the law!

The court's decision made many white people angry. Some of them threatened to use force to stop Black men from voting. Still, in 1866 many Black men in Wisconsin voted for the first time. The election was peaceful.

Women Demand the Right to Vote

At first, the Wisconsin Constitution denied women the right to vote, too. The right to vote is known as suffrage (**suhf** rij).

These suffragists spread their message during a Fourth of July parade in 1912 in Oshkosh.

Women who fought for the right to vote were called suffragists (**suhf** ri jists). Suffragists held conventions in Janesville in 1867 and Milwaukee in 1869. Some of these women organized the Wisconsin Woman Suffrage Association. They set up local chapters in many cities. But they were not very successful. Most people still refused to accept that women could do more than take care of their families and homes.

Suffragists finally had some success in 1885. That year, the legislature passed a law giving women the right to vote in school elections. But they could not vote in other elections. Still, suffragists did not stop. For years they argued that the right to vote should be equal for men and women. Suffragists in Wisconsin marched in parades. They spent time and money to convince people that women should have the right to vote.

bill: Proposed law

Finally, the Wisconsin legislature passed a **bill** that would grant women full voting rights. But voters would have to approve the bill in the November 1912 election. In the months before the vote, suffragists traveled around the state. They mailed pamphlets to voters, asking them to support votes for women. Suffragists went to every county fair and all kinds of meetings. They hoped voters would understand that women deserved the right to vote. In the election, 135,545 people voted to give women the right to vote. But 227,024 voted against it. The bill had failed.

It was a big disappointment to Wisconsin's suffragists, but they kept working. They finally won their victory on a national level. In 1919, suffragists convinced members of the US Congress to approve an amendment to the US Constitution. It would give women the right to vote across the nation.

Next, suffragists had to convince the legislatures in at least 36 states. Those states had to approve the amendment, too. In June 1919, the Wisconsin legislature approved the suffrage amendment. A messenger rushed the papers to Washington, DC. Wisconsin became the first state to ratify, or officially approve, the US Constitution's Nineteenth Amendment. By 1920, women across the nation had the right to vote.

Native People and the Question of Citizenship

Native nations in Wisconsin have their own sovereign governments. Because of that, for a long time most Native people were not US citizens. They were only citizens of their nations. However, Native people could ask Congress to become US citizens.

In the 1830s, citizens of the Brothertown Nation asked to become US citizens to avoid being forced to leave the Wisconsin Territory. In 1839 all Brothertown people were declared US citizens. This meant the US government no longer recognized Brothertown as a sovereign nation. Some Stockbridge-Munsee people also became US citizens in 1843.

Native people who became US citizens had the right to vote in US elections. But they also had to give up their rights as citizens of a sovereign Native nation. Many Native people later chose to give up their US citizenship. Some Stockbridge-Munsee people gave up US citizenship to regain their rights as citizens of their Native nation. The Brothertown people tried to do the same, but they were not successful. Today, the Brothertown Nation has its own government. However, the US government does not recognize the Brothertown Nation as sovereign. Even today, Brothertown continues its fight to regain federal recognition.

The turning point in Native peoples' US citizenship came during World War I (1914–1918). Native people who were not US citizens could not be made to fight in the war. Yet an estimated 12,000 Native people signed up to fight anyway. Many of those were from Wisconsin. The Nineteenth Amendment had given women the right to vote starting in 1920. After that, many people thought it was unfair that all Native people did not have that right.

In 1924, Congress passed the Indian Citizenship Act. This law made all Native people citizens of the US. Since then, members of Native nations have been citizens of the

Native veterans at the Lac Courte Oreilles reservation after returning from World War I

US *and* of their Native nations. The Indian Citizenship Act also gave Native people the right to vote in US elections. Since the Nineteenth Amendment had already passed, Native women could also vote.

Native nations did not have a say in the Indian Citizenship Act. Congress did not let Native nations decide whether they wanted their members to be US citizens. The law made that decision for them. Some Native people did not want to be US citizens. They chose not to vote in US elections. But other Native people did.

Remember the *Simpson Street Free Press* writers from chapter 2? Many of those students have written about issues in their community. For some, that work has led to more opportunities to get involved. A student writer named Kadjata got involved in a local election even though she wasn't old enough to vote in it. The election was for Madison's school board.

School boards make decisions for all of the public schools in a community. Members of a school board are elected by the people. The **candidates** (**kan** di dayts) who run for school board must make sure that voters know their opinions about school issues. How would they fix the challenges facing their community's schools? What do they think is most important for K–12 students? Most students do not get a chance to speak with school board candidates. During Madison's 2022 school board election, one student did.

candidates: People running for office

Kadjata was in high school at the time. She had written articles for the *Simpson Street Free Press* about school issues. She had done lots of research and formed strong opinions. Now, she wanted to know what the candidates thought. Kadjata joined a group of adult reporters in a question-and-answer session. The reporters got to ask all three candidates the same questions. Kadjata asked about topics that mattered to her. How would each candidate make sure all students got the support they needed at school? How should Madison schools measure student progress in reading?

"Do you agree that the right to read is guaranteed in the United States Constitution?"

– One of Kadjata's questions to school board candidates

All three candidates answered Kadjata's questions. This was helpful to the voters who watched the session. It gave them a better idea of who they might want to vote for. Kadjata couldn't vote in the school board election. Still, her voice was part of the process.

CHAPTER 4

State and Tribal Government

The Tribble brothers are members of the Lac Courte Oreilles Band of Lake Superior Chippewa. Where is the Lac Courte Oreilles reservation located? What part of the state do the ceded territories cover? What else does the map show?

In this chapter, you'll learn about each branch of Wisconsin's state government. You'll also learn how Native nations in Wisconsin set up their governments.

Native nations signed treaties with the US government during the 1800s. Those treaties promised the Native nations certain rights. But at times, Wisconsin's state government has failed to uphold the rights of Native nations. Some Tribal citizens have taken action to defend their rights.

In 1837, 1842, and 1854, leaders of Ojibwe nations in Wisconsin signed treaties with the US. The

US government often used threats to force those nations to cede, or give up, most of their land. As a result of the 1854 treaty, the Ojibwe created four reservations: Bad River, Lac Courte Oreilles, Lac du Flambeau, and Red Cliff. But all three treaties said that the Ojibwe would keep their right to hunt, fish, and gather on ceded lands. This included lands that had once been theirs outside of reservations.

For decades, the state of Wisconsin ignored those rights. Law enforcement officers arrested and jailed Ojibwe people who hunted, fished, and gathered on ceded land. In the 1970s, brothers Fred and Mike Tribble of Lac Courte Oreilles took action. They went fishing on part of a lake that was on ceded territory. They knew they might be arrested, and they were. The Tribble brothers fought back through the court system. In the end, the Tribble brothers won their case. In 1983, a federal court upheld the Ojibwe people's treaty rights.

Questions to Think About

- **What does each of the three branches of state government do?**
- **How do the branches work together to strengthen democracy in Wisconsin?**
- **How are Tribal governments similar to and different from state government?**

The Legislative Branch

The writers of the Wisconsin Constitution decided that our state's government would have three branches. Those branches are legislative, executive, and judicial. This followed the pattern of the US Constitution. The federal government has the same three branches. Almost all other states copied this way of organizing government.

The legislative branch is the law-making branch of state government. It creates laws that everyone in the state must follow. The legislative branch has two different houses. They are the senate and the assembly (uh **sem** blee). Members of these houses serve the people who live in their

The Wisconsin State Capitol is home to all three branches of state government. It is located in the capital city of Madison. Notice the spelling! When it is a building, *capitol* is spelled with an *o*. When it is a city, *capital* is spelled with an *a*.

district (**di** strikt). A district is the part of the state they represent. Now look at the table. What are the differences between the two houses?

The Two Houses of the Wisconsin State Legislature		
	Senate	**Assembly**
What are the members called?	Senators	Representatives
How many members are there?	33 One for each senate district in the state	99 One for each assembly district in the state
How long is a member's term?	4 years	2 years

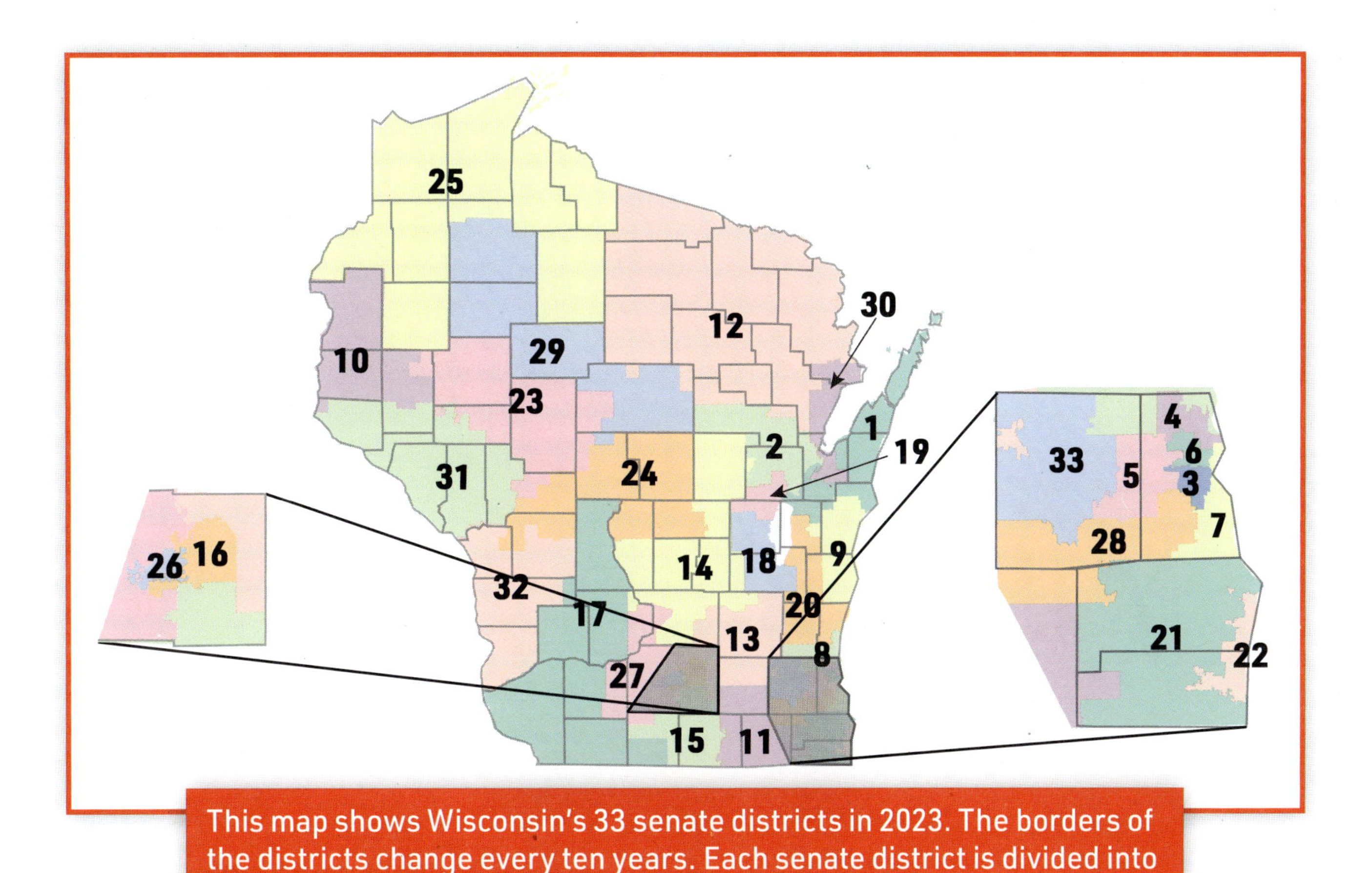

This map shows Wisconsin's 33 senate districts in 2023. The borders of the districts change every ten years. Each senate district is divided into three assembly districts. That makes a total of 99 assembly districts.

This photo shows two representatives from the Wisconsin State Assembly, Jim Steineke and Shelia Stubbs. They wore masks to stay safe during the COVID-19 pandemic.

Members of both houses can suggest new laws. These suggested laws are called bills. Members debate each bill. Then they approve them or turn them down. When suggesting and debating bills, legislators think about the needs of the people in their districts. They also think about the needs of the people throughout the state.

Why does the legislature have two houses instead of one? Having two houses makes the legislature more democratic. Both houses have to pass a bill before it can become a law. This gives people around the state a chance to tell their legislators what they think about the bill. Because leaders in the assembly and the senate debate the same bill, it gets a lot of attention.

Why is lots of attention good? Debating a bill takes many hours. This gives legislators time to think through the bill. Both houses have a chance to make changes or catch mistakes.

Having two houses in the legislature also keeps legislators in touch with their people. Wisconsin has 99 assembly districts and 33 senate districts. That means each representative represents fewer people than each senator. This makes it easier for each representative to know the issues that matter to the people in their district. Because senate districts are larger, senators have to represent more people. It's a little like at school. Like representatives, teachers know a lot about each student in their classrooms. Like senators, the principal may know a little about each student in the whole school. A principal can ask the teacher if they need to know something about any one student.

population: The total number of people living in a certain place

Senate and assembly districts change every ten years. Why? Districts are supposed to be equal in **population** (pop yuh **lay** shun). Keeping the districts equal in population helps keep representation fair. What if 100 people lived in one district and 100,000 people lived in another? Then one representative would have to meet the needs of only 100 people. The other representative would have to meet the

These maps show the shape and size of senate districts 12 and 22 in 2023. District 12 is much larger than district 22. But both districts are home to a similar number of people.

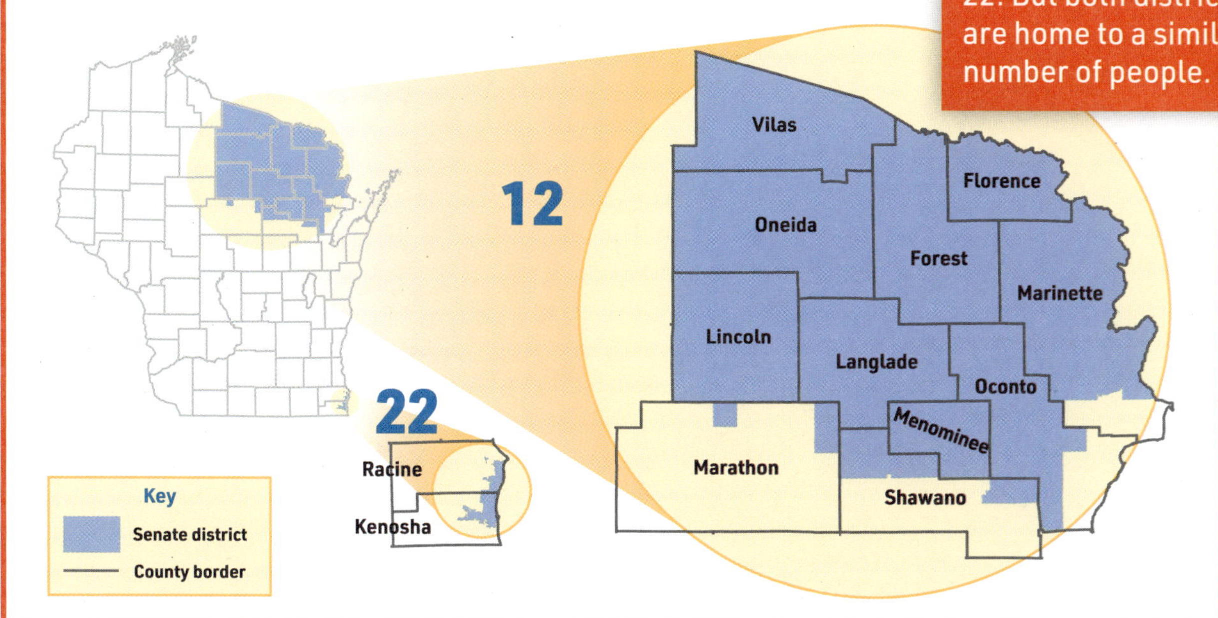

needs of 100,000 people! That wouldn't be fair. The people in the two districts would not have an equal voice.

Over time, some districts gain population. Other districts lose population. As these changes happen, the representation in those districts becomes unequal. Changes must be made. Each person and community should have an equal voice in the legislature.

Every ten years the US government takes a census (**sen** suhs). That's when the government hires people to count everybody who lives in the country. After the census, we know each area's population. We can see how unequal a state's districts have become. The legislature must redraw the districts to keep their populations closer to equal. This process is called redistricting (ree **di** strikt ing). If a state does not redistrict every ten years, the differences between districts keep growing.

The Executive Branch

The governor heads the executive branch of Wisconsin's government. A governor is elected every four years. In Wisconsin, there is no limit to the number of terms any one person can serve as governor. The governor represents all the people in the state and enforces state laws. But the governor cannot do everything. Governors appoint people to manage the major state **agencies** (**ay** juhn seez). This includes the Department of Health Services and the Department of Natural Resources, among others. The governor also suggests new laws to the legislature. And after both houses of the legislature have passed a bill, the governor can sign it to make it a law. Or, the governor can veto (**vee** toh), or say no to, the bill. Then it does not become law.

agencies: Government departments that provide services to the public

Governor Martin Schreiber signs an education bill into law in front of a group of young people. Schreiber was governor of Wisconsin from 1977 to 1979.

The Wisconsin Constitution created other executive officers to help the governor. The writers of the constitution thought these jobs were so important that the voters should elect them.

- The lieutenant governor is the state's "second-in-command." This person carries out the duties of the governor if the governor is out of state. If the governor dies or leaves office, the lieutenant governor becomes governor.

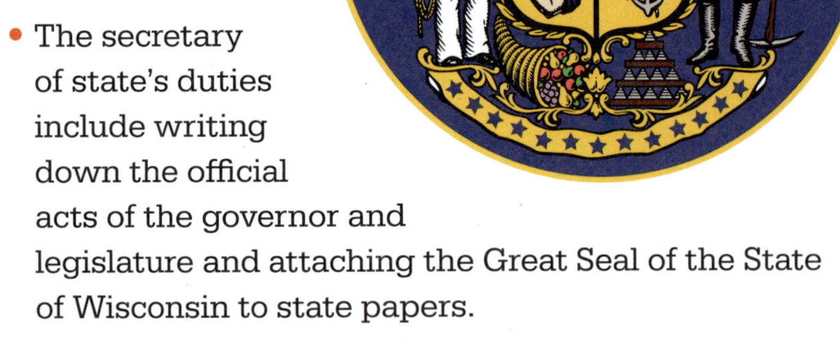

The Great Seal of Wisconsin was created in 1881. It contains many state symbols. Which symbols do you notice? Why do you think they appear on the seal?

- The secretary of state's duties include writing down the official acts of the governor and legislature and attaching the Great Seal of the State of Wisconsin to state papers.
- The attorney general represents the state in court, provides legal advice to the governor and other state officials, and enforces state laws.
- The state treasurer manages the state's money.
- The superintendent of public instruction leads the state's public school system.

The Judicial Branch

What happens when someone is accused of breaking the law? Or when people cannot settle a disagreement involving the law? What if someone's constitutional rights are denied? In all these cases, the judicial branch gets involved. Judges make up the judicial branch of government. State court judges resolve disagreements between people. They do this by applying state law to the facts of a case.

State judges oversee trials. There are different kinds of trials. A criminal trial is held when someone is charged with a crime. A criminal trial might be held before a judge or a jury. In a criminal trial, a person is found guilty or not guilty. A person found guilty of a crime has a right to **appeal** (uh **peel**) their case.

appeal: To ask that a decision made by a court of law be changed

Civil (**siv** uhl) trials are held for disagreements that do not involve crimes. In a civil case, a judge or jury decides which side wins. Civil cases can also be appealed.

The judicial branch of state government has courts at three levels:

- The lowest level is the circuit (**sur** kit) court.
- The middle level is the court of appeals.
- The top level is the supreme court.

Being at the lowest level does not mean circuit courts are least important. It means that cases start at that level. Each county has at least one circuit court branch. When someone is accused of a crime, their case is filed in a circuit court. If the case goes to trial, a circuit court judge or jury determines the facts of the case and makes a decision. Circuit judges and juries can also hear civil cases.

The Wisconsin Constitution gives every person charged with a crime the right to a trial by jury. Every person charged with a crime also has the right to be defended in court by a lawyer. In court, there are always two sides represented. On one side, a lawyer represents the defendant (dif **en** duhnt), the person accused of breaking the law. On the other side, a district attorney acts as the prosecutor (**pross** uh kyoo tur). The district attorney represents the state.

In court, the district attorney presents arguments and evidence against the defendant. The defendant's lawyer presents arguments and evidence in favor of the defendant. The judge and jury listen to both sides. The jury then meets to decide whether the defendant is guilty or not guilty based on the facts of the case. But that is not always where the story ends.

A defendant found guilty of a crime can appeal the decision to the next highest level. After circuit court, the next level is the Wisconsin Court of Appeals. That court reviews the case. It decides whether or not the circuit court trial was handled according to the law. The decision may still seem unfair to the defendant. If so, they can make one more appeal. They can ask the Wisconsin Supreme Court to review the lower court's decision. The supreme court does not have to take every case. It reviews only a small number of cases.

Judges for the supreme court are called justices. The Wisconsin Supreme Court has seven justices. Each justice is elected to a ten-year term. Supreme court justices elect one of their members to be the chief justice. That person is responsible for running the court.

The supreme court also settles disagreements over the meaning of the state constitution. For example, the

The seven Wisconsin Supreme Court justices in 2022. From left to right: Justices Brian Hagedorn, Rebecca Grassl Bradley, Ann Walsh Bradley, Annette Kingsland Ziegler, Patience D. Roggensack, Rebecca Frank Dallet, and Jill J. Karofsky

Wisconsin Constitution says that the police cannot search your private property without permission from a judge. In the 1980s, police officers searched a man's garbage without permission. That man went to court. His case made it all the way to the Wisconsin Supreme Court. The supreme court decided that garbage put out on the curb is not private property. The police are allowed to search through it without permission from a judge.

Checks and Balances

The people who wrote the Wisconsin Constitution and the voters who approved it divided state government into three branches. They gave each branch its own responsibilities. But they also made sure that no branch could become too powerful. They gave each branch a way to "check," or limit, the other branch's power. These checks allow the three branches of government to stay in balance. This system of "checks and balances" keeps all three branches responsible to the citizens of Wisconsin.

How do these checks and balances work? Look closely at the diagram to find out.

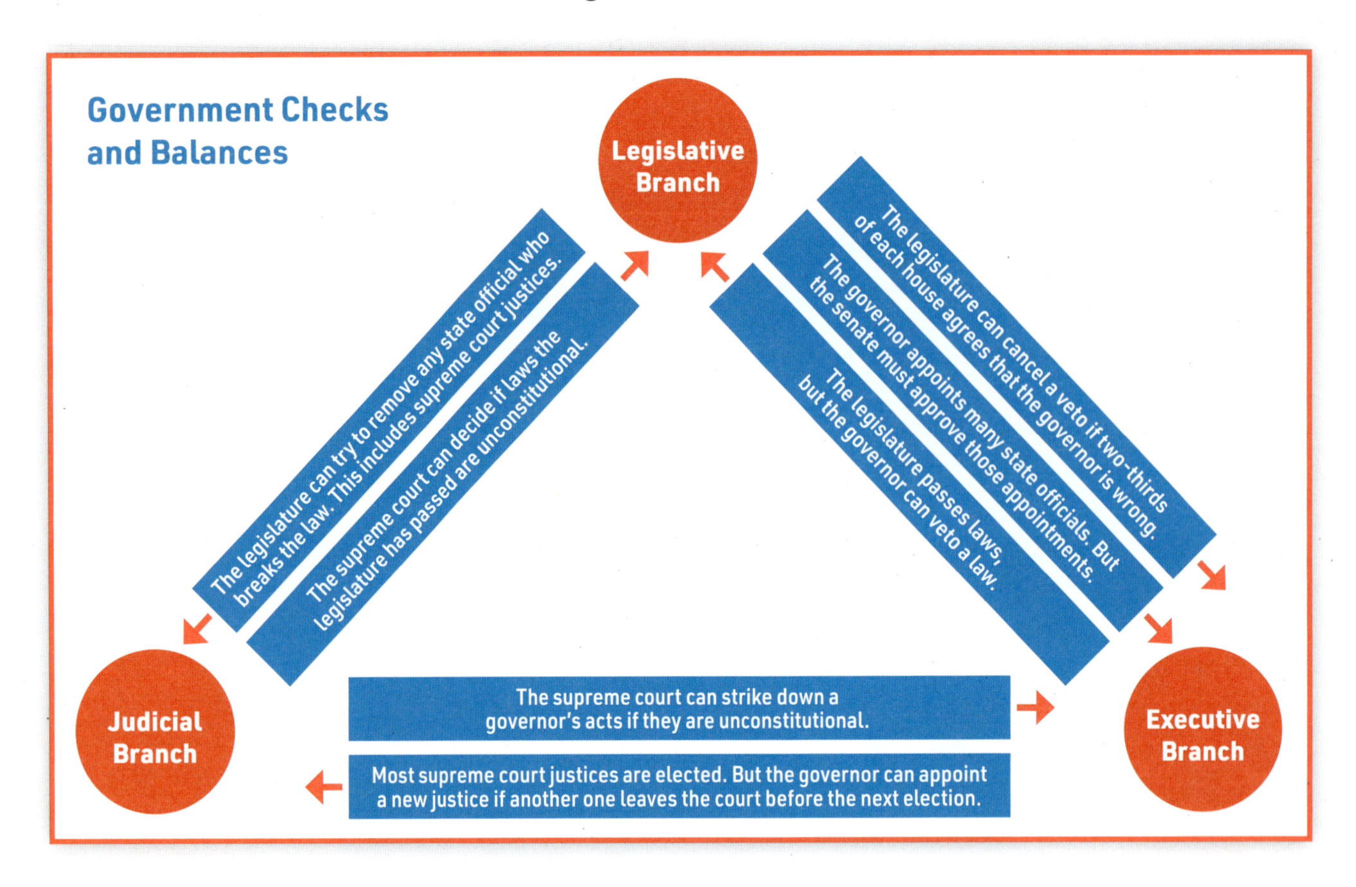

Tribal Governments

Native nations including those in Wisconsin have their own governments. Each Native nation also has its own constitution. That constitution describes how its Tribal government will work.

Some Tribal governments are similar in structure to Wisconsin's state government. Others are different. The Ho-Chunk government includes four branches, not three. It has executive, legislative, and judicial branches. It also has

Each of the Native nations in Wisconsin has its own flag. The 11 federally recognized nations' flags stand inside the State Capitol building. In this photo you can see six of them: (left to right) the Ho-Chunk, Lac du Flambeau, Oneida, Stockbridge-Munsee, Forest County Potawatomi, and Menominee flags.

a general council. The Ho-Chunk General Council includes all citizens of the nation.

Tribal governments work a lot like other democratic governments. Tribal citizens elect a legislature. The Tribal legislature passes laws that affect Tribal citizens and non-Native people. Each Native nation has an executive branch that enforces those laws. The executive branch also provides services for Tribal citizens. Native nations in Wisconsin call their executive branch a Tribal council, Tribal governing board, or business committee. The elected leader of the executive branch is either the chairperson or president. Each of the Native nations in Wisconsin also has a judicial branch to decide disagreements between Tribal citizens. Most of the 12 nations have courts, but not all do.

Each Tribal government in Wisconsin also works to preserve its nation's history and culture. Most Native nations have a Tribal historian. Their job is to keep the traditional histories of the nation and teach them to the children. Preserving culture and language is a very important part of Tribal sovereignty and government.

GETTING INVOLVED

For decades, people have called for an end to the use of race-based mascots. This includes mascots based on stereotypes of Native people. This kind of mascot is harmful to Native and non-Native people. Some members of the Wisconsin state legislature decided to do something about it. In 2009, they introduced a bill. The bill would make school leaders prove that their mascot did not lead to unfair treatment, harassment, or stereotyping of any group. If school leaders could not prove that, then the school had to stop using the mascot.

"I have been living on the Menominee Reservation all my life. I care about this issue because it impacts me directly seeing as how I am a Native American myself. I find the portraying of Native Americans as mascots extremely disrespectful. I think the Native American mascots should be banned. I think the assembly should pass the bill. The reason I think this is because they do nothing but stereotype us."

—Shawn, a student at Menominee Nation High School (then called Menominee Indian High School)

Before a bill can become a state law, members of the legislature have to vote on it. Before that vote happens, members of the public can share their opinions with legislators at public hearings. At these hearings, people stand up and speak directly to their legislators. They share their opinions. They tell their stories. This helps legislators better understand how a bill might affect the people they represent.

Some students at Menominee Nation High School in Keshena wanted schools to stop using race-based mascots. They especially didn't like mascots that were disrespectful to Native nations like theirs. They supported the bill. They wanted state legislators to hear their thoughts before voting on the bill. So the students shared their opinions at a public hearing.

Another group of students in a different part of the state also felt strongly about this issue. The students at Prescott High School were not citizens of a Native nation. But they had taken a class on Native history at school. The class got them interested in the mascot issue. They heard about the state legislature's bill. Then, they decided to share their opinions at a public hearing.

These students made a difference by speaking up and getting involved. The assembly and senate both passed the bill. In 2010, Governor Jim Doyle signed it into law.

"I and my friends have come here today asking that you help stop the use of race-based mascots in our public schools. This issue is all about cultural respect."

– Sarah, a student at Prescott High School

CHAPTER 5

Government Working for the People

The governor is responsible for enforcing state laws. The governor also runs the state. That includes providing services such as education, clean water, and road repairs. Lots of people help the governor provide these services. Many of them work for state agencies that serve the people of Wisconsin.

Sometimes, state agencies need help. They need people to speak up when they see that individuals or groups are not getting the services they need. In the 1960s, a man named Jesus Salas did just that.

Jesus Salas speaks to migrant farmworkers in Wautoma, Wisconsin, in 1968.

In winter and spring, Salas and his family lived in Texas. During the summer and fall, they traveled to Wisconsin to work on farms. Many other families in Texas and Mexico did the same. These people are called migrant farmworkers. Salas knew how dangerous work on the farms could be. He saw that some employers did not treat migrant farmworkers fairly. He chose to do something about it.

Salas led farmworkers in protests and marches. He also spoke to people in state agencies. For example, he told the Wisconsin Employment Relations Commission (WERC) about the unsafe, unfair working conditions he had seen. WERC tries to resolve problems between employers and workers. Salas convinced government officials to do more for migrant farmworkers. He helped to improve working conditions for many people.

Questions to Think About

- **What do state agencies do?**
- **How do state agencies keep people safe?**
- **How do state agencies provide people with equal opportunities?**

How Can State Agencies Respond to People's Needs?

commission: A group of people directed to perform some duty

In this chapter, you will learn about some of the many state agencies and **commissions** (kuh **mi** shuhnz). You'll learn what they do for the people of Wisconsin. You'll see how state government has responded to people's changing needs by providing more services over the years.

Protecting Workers

Some state agencies are responsible for making workplaces safe and fair. They promote equal work opportunities for people across the state. In the 1960s, Jesus Salas worked with some of them, such as the Wisconsin Employment Relations Commission. That group still exists today.

The Department of Workforce Development is another agency that protects workers. It helps people who have lost their jobs and those who have been injured at work. It helps people learn new skills and find new jobs. It enforces work-related laws, such as those that govern:

- The jobs young people are allowed to have
- How much people must be paid for their work
- How groups with special needs are treated at work, such as migrant farmworkers, veterans, and people with disabilities

This photo was taken in 1931 in Madison. The teacher and her students are listening to a radio. This was a common way to get the news at that time. Where do most people get their news today? How can paying attention to the news help us think about and debate different points of view?

Teaching the People

In a democracy, everyone has the right to an education. In school, students like you learn the rights and responsibilities that are key to a democracy. You learn to think about and debate different points of view. You learn about your own community and others.

Since 1848, the state of Wisconsin has provided public education. The state constitution created the Office of the Superintendent of Public Instruction. This office required the legislature to create public schools. Anyone aged 4–20 could attend those schools for free. Today this office is called the Department of Public Instruction (DPI). It is led by the state superintendent. DPI provides training and resources to teachers and libraries. It sets standards for graduation. But the DPI does not run every school in Wisconsin. That's up to the local government.

This photo was taken at UW–Madison's spring 2022 graduation ceremony.

Wisconsin's early leaders saw the need to provide even more education to the people. In 1848, the legislature started the University of Wisconsin in Madison. In 1854, the University of Wisconsin awarded degrees to its first class. There were only two graduates! Today the University of Wisconsin has locations around the state.

In the early 1900s, university president Charles Van Hise and Governor Robert La Follette created the "Wisconsin Idea." They believed that the university and state government should work together for the good of everyone in the state. In 1893, the University of Wisconsin–Extension was created to "extend" classes to everyone. Anyone in the state who was interested could learn more about any subject. Experts from the universities could also give advice to government officials on subjects they knew a lot about.

Through the Extension program, professors traveled to towns and cities to give lectures. Experts from the UW College of Agriculture gave advice to farmers. Today, the University of Wisconsin continues to provide education to people around the state. Extension has programs for young people, too. These include camps, afterschool programs, and clubs like Wisconsin 4-H.

Another state agency that provides educational services is the Educational Communications Board. It works with UW–Madison to broadcast Wisconsin Public Radio and PBS Wisconsin. These broadcasts bring educational programs to people's homes and classrooms across the state.

These women are taking a carpentry class offered by UW–Extension around the year 1900.

In these photos, DATCP workers inspect a meat slicer at the grocery store and honeybee hives. Why is it important to make sure these things are safe?

Keeping Business Safe and Fair

When you buy food at the grocery store, you expect it to be safe to eat, right? And your parents expect that when they buy a new car, it will run. The Department of Agriculture, Trade and Consumer Protection (DATCP) helps make sure things people buy are safe. Since farming has always been important in the state, this protection began with farm products. In 1839, the Wisconsin Territory's assembly required every county to have an inspector. The inspector made sure food products like milk and cheese were healthy and safe.

Since the 1970s, DATCP has protected more than just our food. The department prevents false advertising and unsafe products. It creates rules that protect us from people who might produce or sell goods and services unfairly.

Keeping People Healthy

The Wisconsin Department of Health Services (DHS) also helps keep people in Wisconsin healthy and safe. It has programs to help people maintain their physical and mental health. It monitors certain health care providers. This helps to make sure people get good care. DHS also helps people with low incomes, elderly people, and people with disabilities get health care. And it lets people know how to avoid contagious diseases.

Protecting Our Resources

Wisconsin has outstanding natural resources. We have beautiful forests, lakes and streams, fish, and game animals. Our state also has mineral resources such as iron ore, limestone, and lead. The Wisconsin Department of Natural Resources (DNR) protects these resources from pollution and misuse. The DNR provides ways for everyone to enjoy our natural resources. It also makes sure that outdoor sports such as hunting and fishing are done in a way that will not harm the environment.

Each year, the Wisconsin DNR holds a sticker design contest. High school students can submit their designs. This was the winning design in 2023. People can buy a sticker to put on their car window. The sticker gets them into all of the state parks. Did you know that the DNR manages all of Wisconsin's state parks? Have you visited any of them? If you could design a state park sticker, what would it look like?

Travel Around the State

tourism: Travel for pleasure

Tourism (**tur** iz uhm) is very important to Wisconsin. The state's Department of Tourism promotes travel to Wisconsin. The Department of Tourism has travel information centers. There, visitors can learn more about where to go in the state. The department also creates advertisements and publications that are sent to other states to encourage people to visit Wisconsin.

Do you recognize the man in these photos? Donald Driver played football for the Green Bay Packers for 14 seasons. Which popular Wisconsin activities is he participating in? Do you think this ad convinced many people to visit Wisconsin?

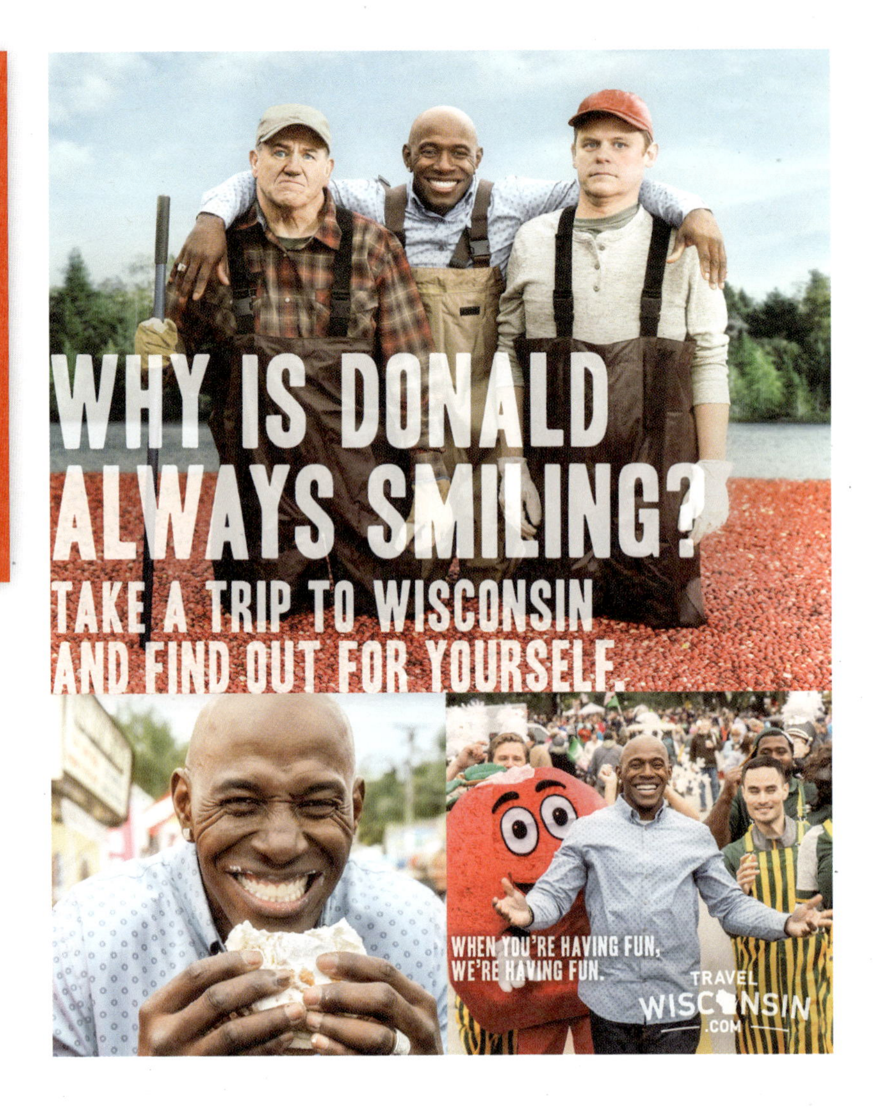

Traveling around the state requires good roads. In 1911, the legislature created the State Highway Commission to build public highways. More and more people began driving automobiles on roads and highways. The state recognized a need to promote safe driving. Today, the Department of Transportation does many things to keep us safe on the roads. This includes:

- Planning and constructing roads and highways
- Promoting highway safety
- Enforcing traffic laws through the state patrol
- Issuing driver's licenses
- Registering vehicles

State Agencies and Tribal Governments Work Together

Tribal governments provide many services to their citizens. But remember that Native people are also citizens of the US and the states they live in. Native people have the right to receive state services as well. In 2004, Wisconsin governor Jim Doyle told state agencies to work more closely with Native nations. The goal was to improve the services that state agencies provide to citizens of Native nations. This also strengthened the government-to-government relationship between the state and Native nations.

GETTING INVOLVED

Would you like to help protect Wisconsin's land, waters, and wildlife? One way is to share your voice with the Wisconsin **Conservation** (**kon** sur vay shuhn) Congress. In our federal government, Congress is a group of elected legislators. Those legislators make our nation's laws. The Wisconsin Conservation Congress (WCC) is different. Wisconsin citizens can elect people to the WCC, but the WCC does not make laws. Instead, the group shares ideas with the DNR about how to protect our state's natural resources. Maybe you see something that is harming the land, water, or wildlife where you live. You might have an idea for how to change that. Share your idea with the WCC! People of all ages can suggest ideas.

conservation: The protection of natural resources like land, water, and wildlife

During an event called the Spring Hearings, members of the public can vote on the ideas people have suggested. This includes you! You do not have to be 18 to vote in the WCC's Spring Hearings. The WCC and DNR send some of those ideas to the state legislature. The legislature could turn those ideas into new state laws! This process lets everyone share their voice on conservation issues in Wisconsin.

Young people in Wisconsin can also join the Youth Conservation Congress, or YCC. The YCC is a special program of the WCC. The young people who join learn about conservation laws. They help with conservation projects. YCC members have counted wildlife. They have checked the quality of air and water. They have improved their hunting, fishing, and gathering skills. The YCC is for anyone under age 18. The youngest participant so far was only eight!

Have you heard of the Great Lakes Indian Fish and Wildlife Commission, or GLIFWC? This group represents 11 Ojibwe nations in Wisconsin, Minnesota, and Michigan. Like the DNR, GLIFWC helps protect our natural resources. The group also teaches people about treaty rights. This includes Tribal citizens' rights to hunt, fish, and gather on ceded lands.

GLIFWC has a summer camp for young Tribal citizens called Onji-Akiing. The name is Ojibwe for "From the Earth." Campers complete projects to take care of their environment. They have planted trees and pollinator gardens. They have improved trails and made signs about native plants. Campers also learn about natural resources jobs. They make traditional crafts, listen to Ojibwe Elders, and take part in ceremonial activities. Campers at Onji-Akiing spend time in nature. They learn the traditional ways their people have interacted with nature. And they learn how they can help preserve nature for the future.

"I was able to watch and hold a cow elk as the DNR and Rocky Mountain Elk Foundation were tranquilizing them and then collaring and taking measurements. It was the coolest experience, but I got a lot of elk drool on my pants."

–YCC participant from La Crosse

Local Government

municipal: Having to do with a city or town and its services

In this chapter, you will learn about county and **municipal** (myoo **nis** uh puhl) government. You'll learn about how local governments keep people safe, provide equal opportunities, and solve problems.

In the 1950s, Vel Phillips saw a big problem in Milwaukee. Black people were treated unfairly. They did not have the same opportunities that white people had. They could not live in any neighborhood they chose. People would sell homes or rent apartments to Black people in only a small section of the city. That part of the city was run down. It was overcrowded. The streets were falling apart. Phillips wanted to change things for the

Vel Phillips speaks at the Milwaukee Common Council around 1970.

better. She decided to join her local government. Phillips ran for the Milwaukee Common Council, and she won. The common council had the power to pass and enforce city laws called ordinances (**or** duh nuhn siz). Ordinances begin as bills that members of the common council vote on. Over and over, Phillips suggested a fair housing bill to the council. Every time, the other council members voted it down. Phillips didn't give up. She kept at it for six years. She teamed up with community leaders. Thousands of people protested, marched, and spoke in favor of fair housing.

In 1968, the president of the United States signed a federal law called the Fair Housing Act. After that, the Milwaukee Common Council finally passed a fair housing ordinance. Black people in Milwaukee had more choices for where to live. And Vel Phillips had helped make it happen.

Questions to Think About

- **How do different levels of government help communities?**
- **How is local government different from state government? How is it similar?**
- **What does county government do?**
- **What responsibilities are left up to cities, villages, and towns?**

Two Kinds of Local Government

Wisconsin is a big state. Its people have many different needs and wants. The people of Green Bay need and want different things than the people of La Crosse. This is why local government is so important. Government at the local level allows people to decide for themselves what services the government should provide. It allows them to solve problems that affect their communities.

There are two basic kinds of local governments: county and municipal. County governments are larger than municipal governments. Cities, villages, and towns are all types of municipal governments. Municipal governments are different depending on a place's population. Cities are the largest. They govern the greatest number of people living close together. Villages are like very small cities. Towns govern fewer people spread out over a large area.

Each type of local government has different responsibilities. Each provides important services to its people. In some ways, your school is similar. Your school district sets rules that all schools in your district must follow. In this way, the school district is like the county level of government. But your school can set its own rules, too.

County Government

Today, the state of Wisconsin is divided into 72 counties. But that number has changed over time.

- 1848: 29 counties
- 1861: 58 counties

CHAPTER 6 | **Local Government**

Wisconsin's last county, Menominee, was created in 1961. It includes the entire Menominee Indian Reservation. Which county do you live in? Can you find it on the map?

- 1901: 71 counties
- 1961: 72 counties (the same number as today)

Counties differ in size and population. Marathon County is the largest of Wisconsin's counties in land area. Pepin County is the smallest. The largest in population is Milwaukee County. The smallest is Menominee County. Can you find all four of those counties on the map?

rural: Having to do with the countryside where not many people live

Each county's population growth rate is different, too. In northern, mostly **rural** (**rur** uhl) counties the population has been going down in recent years. Other counties, like Waukesha and Dane, are growing quickly. More and more people move to them every year.

County governments carry out duties required by the state. The residents of the county elect the sheriff, district attorney, and judges. Every county has a sheriff and deputies to enforce laws and help people in trouble. Each county has its own court and courthouse.

The state requires each county to provide information about the people who live there. This can include information about court trials and taxes. The courthouse makes this information easily available when people need it.

Many counties hold fairs. Members of a community gather at county fairs for food and fun. People can show off farm animals they've raised or produce they've grown. These children are showing their calves at the Walworth County Fair in 1945. Have you ever been to a county fair? What did you do there?

Counties also provide services to local areas. Counties construct and maintain roads called county trunk highways. Each winter, county crews plow those roads so they are safe to drive.

Some counties run employment centers to help people find jobs. Counties have health offices to help people with physical and mental illnesses. People pay for these services through property taxes. Every property owner in the county pays taxes to the government. The county government decides which services to provide with that money.

Each county is divided into districts of equal population. Each of those districts elects a supervisor to sit on the county board. Supervisors in most counties serve two-year terms. In Milwaukee County they serve four-year terms. Counties also have an executive branch of government.

Each county has a "county seat." This is where the business of government is located. It is also home to the county courthouse. People pay their property taxes at the courthouse. The circuit court meets there. Often, the courthouse is where you'll find the sheriff's department and the board of supervisors. The county courthouse is like a capitol building for the county.

Municipal Government

Wisconsin has three different kinds of municipal government: cities, villages, and towns. They provide services like counties do, but for a smaller area.

Cities are units of government for small areas with a large population. There is great variety among cities' populations. Wisconsin's largest city is Milwaukee. In 2020,

Milwaukee (left) is in the southeast part of the state. Bayfield (right) is in the northwest part of the state. How might these two cities be different? What might they have in common? What might the people who live there need and want?

close to 600,000 people lived in Milwaukee. In 2020, the state's smallest city was Bayfield. It had a population of 584 people that year.

People who live close together need to cooperate. They need to share resources more often than people who live far apart. Cities provide more services than towns or villages. In rural areas, most houses are built far apart. Each house has its own well for drinking water. But in cities, homes are built much closer together. Building lots of wells close together isn't safe for the water supply. So cities operate a water system that provides everybody with clean drinking water.

What else do cities do? Here are more examples:

- Enforce laws through police departments
- Have fire departments to fight fires
- Keep city streets in good repair
- Collect garbage and recyclable materials
- Provide public libraries and parks for people to enjoy
- Have rules that keep people from constructing unsafe buildings

Cities have their own three branches of government, just like the state. They are the legislative, executive, and judicial branches. The city council is the legislative branch of city government. It passes ordinances to govern the city. A city is divided into wards (wordz). Wards are combined into districts. Each district is equal in population. Voters in each district elect an alder (**awl** dur) to represent them in the city council.

This is an early photo of the Kilbourn fire department. How does the fire truck in this photo compare to those used today?

Cities have either a mayor or a city manager who heads the executive branch of municipal government. The city's voters elect a mayor. The city council appoints a city manager. The mayor or city manager runs the different departments of city government. They make sure that laws are enforced. Just like the state's governor, a mayor or city manager needs help from other elected officials. The city clerk keeps information about the people who live in the city. The treasurer manages the city's money.

Green Bay's Bay Beach is a special kind of public park. It is an amusement park with rides like the Zippin' Pippin roller coaster. Why do you think the people of Green Bay wanted a park like this in their city? What might your community want for its public parks?

Many cities also have a judicial branch. Municipal courts hold trials for people who break city ordinances, such as parking illegally or speeding. People who break ordinances often must pay a fine to the city.

Villages work a lot like cities, but with a much smaller population. When a few hundred people live close together, they still need services similar to those in a city. But villages

do not need as many people to provide those services. Their governments can be smaller.

Villages have a board of trustees that is made up of three to six members. The voters elect the trustees. Each trustee represents the whole village. Villages do not have mayors. Instead, voters elect a village president. They make sure that laws are enforced and services are provided.

Towns are the third form of local government. The legislative body is the "town meeting." At town meetings, all voting citizens come together. They make decisions about laws and what to spend money on. The day-to-day business of towns is carried out by a town board. Usually a board is made up of three supervisors. Towns have elected officials including a clerk and a treasurer.

Most towns are rural. Towns are large in area and small in population. Town roads connect rural areas and allow people to travel safely. So the most important job of town government is maintaining roads. Towns may also operate centers for people to bring their waste materials to recycle. Larger towns may also provide fire and police services to keep people safe.

School Districts

Students in Wisconsin can attend public, private, or homeschools. Public school districts are a part of municipal government. A school district's job is to provide education. School districts run the public elementary, middle, and high schools in a certain area. Each of Wisconsin's school districts has its own superintendent. The superintendent manages all of the public schools within the district. The superintendent must also report to the school board.

A school board is a group of people who govern all of a district's public schools. Wisconsin's school boards have between 3 and 11 members. All of the members are elected by the people. School boards have many responsibilities. Some of those include:

- Evaluating teachers and principals
- Making sure schools have what they need for students to learn
- Creating safety plans for schools

School boards hold regular meetings to discuss issues and make decisions. The meetings are open to the public. Anyone can attend. People who live in a school district can ask to speak at school board meetings to share their opinion on school matters.

Tribal Government Services

Tribal governments are not the same as local governments. Tribal governments are sovereign. Still, Tribal governments provide many of the same services that local governments do. These services promote the health, safety, and well-being of Tribal citizens. Native nations run their own police departments and health clinics. Some Native nations in Wisconsin run their own schools. For example, the Menominee run their own public K–8 school and a college. Most of the students at Menominee Indian School District are Native. Menominee students can choose to attend public schools, private schools, or homeschools, just as all other students in the state can.

GETTING INVOLVED

The city of Oshkosh had a goal. City officials wanted more people to ride bikes to get around. The local government provided bike trails and bike racks on buses. But not many people knew about these things. The city needed help to spread the word. That's when Rick Leib and his students stepped in.

Mr. Leib is a teacher at Oshkosh North High School. He leads a program called Communities. It's a class that allows students to work on real-life projects. The projects can involve all sorts of communities: global, national, state, local, and school. Students in Mr. Leib's class liked the idea of getting more people to bike in their city. But before they could help, they had to learn more. Mr. Leib's students did research. They found out that biking is good for the environment, people's health, and even local businesses. They took a trip to Madison, which is known for being a bike-friendly city. They asked Madison government leaders how they get people excited about biking. Then, Mr. Leib's students worked with their city government to hold an event. They called it "Bike Osh." It was so popular that now the event happens every year. And every year, students at Oshkosh North High School are in charge.

During Bike Osh, local businesses act as "pit stops." On the day of the event, people bike to as many pit stops as they can. They collect raffle tickets at each stop. At the last stop, they enter their raffle tickets into a drawing to win a prize. Those who participate in the event learn how easy it is to get around on two wheels. Those who don't participate still see cyclists pedaling all over the city. Maybe it inspires some of them to try cycling, too.

"It's been a week since #BikeOsh22 & just over 100 people made biking visible in our city! THANK YOU for contributing to our event & making our community stronger. We cannot wait for the next #BikeOsh23! Keep riding Oshkosh!"

– From the student-run Bike Osh Facebook page

Mr. Leib's high school students are responsible for every part of the event. Here are some things they do:

- Visit businesses to ask if they want to be pit stops.
- Write social media posts to let people know about the event.
- Go to local radio stations to make commercials about it.
- Decorate the pit stops.
- Hand out raffle tickets and cheer bikers on during the event.
- Hand out awards at the end of the event.

Being involved with Bike Osh has gotten many students interested in cycling, too. Some students in Mr. Leib's class get together for Saturday morning bike rides. They have a friendly competition to see who has cycled the most miles. Mr. Leib's students have discovered that getting involved with their city can be fun. It can lead them to new interests and experiences. And it can help them make a big difference in their city.

Students at Roosevelt Middle School of the Arts in Milwaukee saw a problem in their neighborhood. Too many people were driving unsafely near their school. People walking on the sidewalk and crossing the street were in danger. At least one student had been hit by a car. Others were afraid they would be, too.

Santanna Dillon was a sixth-grade teacher at Roosevelt Middle School. She and her students decided to do something. They wrote letters to Milwaukee's mayor, Cavalier Johnson. In their letters, they told the mayor how dangerous driving affected them. They asked the city government to do something to stop it. They even suggested ways to fix the problem.

After he received their letters, Mayor Johnson visited the sixth graders at school. He answered their questions. He explained what the city was doing to solve the dangerous driving problem. City leaders were adding protected bike lanes to roads. They were adding more space between cars and sidewalks. They were trying out ways to slow cars down. The students were glad that the city took their concerns seriously.

Maybe you have noticed a problem in your community. Maybe you have an idea that could make your community safer, cleaner, healthier, or more fun. If so, speak up! Take action! You can have a big impact on your community.

"I think that they should have a police officer in every school parking lot."

"To help this problem they should have a more advanced driving test."

"A way to fix that problem is to move up the age of when you can start driving from 16 to 18."

– From letters Ms. Dillon's students wrote to the mayor

CHAPTER 7

Political Parties and Elections

political: Having to do with politics, or the debates and activities among people and groups about how to govern

Many adults belong to **political** (puh **lit** uh kuhl) parties. Political parties are made up of people who share similar ideas of what government should do. When some people aren't happy with the political parties that exist, they can create a new one. This happened in Wisconsin in the 1800s.

In 1854, the two main political parties in the US were the Democrats and the Whigs. At that time, slavery was still legal in many parts of the country. New states and territories were still being formed in the west. Some of them allowed slavery. Others did not. The Democrats believed the people of each state or territory should decide whether to allow slavery. Whigs were divided on the question. Some Whigs believed the US should do away with slavery completely. Other Whigs disagreed.

The 1854 gathering in Ripon took place at this building. Back then, it was a schoolhouse. Today, it is a museum.

In Wisconsin, a group of people gathered in the town of Ripon. They were not happy with the Democrats or the Whigs. They wanted to make sure slavery would not be allowed in the new territories and states. So they helped form a new political party. They called it the Republican Party. The Republican Party soon became powerful. It spread across the country.

After the 1854 meeting at the Ripon schoolhouse, similar meetings happened in other states. Soon people organized a national Republican Party. By 1860, most people in Wisconsin's state government were members of the Republican Party. The Democrats were still powerful, too. The Whig party had disappeared. During the Civil War (1861–1865), most Wisconsinites fought to stop the spread of slavery.

In this chapter, you'll learn about another political party that formed in Wisconsin. You'll learn about how political parties affect elections. And you'll learn about the different kinds of elections that are held in Wisconsin.

Questions to Think About

- **What do political parties do?**
- **Why might someone join a political party?**
- **Why might someone form a new political party?**
- **How do national, state, and local elections work in Wisconsin?**
- **How do Tribal government elections work?**

Political Parties in Wisconsin

nominate: Suggest someone for a job, political position, or honor

A political party helps candidates get elected. Political parties **nominate** (**nahm** uh nayt) a candidate for a certain office. They work to get their candidate elected. They might run ads on TV, radio, and the internet. Sometimes they go door-to-door to talk to voters. People often vote for a candidate because of that candidate's political party.

Since the 1950s, the voting population in Wisconsin has been close to half Democrat and half Republican. But they are not the only two political parties in Wisconsin. Sometimes, voters feel that the Democrats and Republicans do not pay attention to things that are important to them. So they organize a new political party. Today, the other most popular parties in Wisconsin are:

- Libertarian (lib ur **tair** ee uhn) Party
- Green Party
- Constitution Party

The Democratic Party's color is blue. Its symbol is a donkey. The Republican Party's color is red. Its symbol is an elephant. These colors and symbols are used on yard signs, posters, buttons, ads, and even political cartoons. Where have you seen them?

Robert "Fighting Bob" La Follette in 1906

The Progressive Movement

The most successful political effort in the early 1900s was the Progressive (pruh **gre** siv) movement. Progressives supported progress, or positive change. The most famous Progressive leader in Wisconsin was Robert La Follette. He fought so hard for change that people called him "Fighting Bob." La Follette was a member of the Republican Party. He wanted to make the Republican Party and the state government more willing to answer to the people of the state. Many people in the party disliked La Follette's ideas. For many years the Progressives remained a separate group within the Republican Party.

In 1900, La Follette was elected governor. He served until 1906, when he became a US senator. Under La Follette and others, the Progressives fought for laws and programs that:

- Made businesses and industries treat employees more fairly
- Made workplaces safer
- Made sure businesses charged fair prices
- Helped workers who were hurt on the job
- Helped those who had lost their jobs

In 1934, the Progressives left the Republican Party. They formed a separate political party. After early success, support for the Progressive Party began to drop in the 1940s. Many of its younger members joined the Democratic Party.

Elections in Wisconsin

In a democracy, people elect the officials who serve in government. Voters in Wisconsin participate in different kinds of elections. Some elections are partisan (**pahr** ti zuhn). This means candidates run as members of a political party. Other elections are nonpartisan. In nonpartisan elections, candidates may or may not be members of a political party. But they do not represent a political party during the election.

What happens if two people from the same political party run for the same office? A primary election is held. Before the primary election, people who want to run for office ask others to help nominate them. If they get enough support, they become candidates in the primary election. Their names will appear on the ballot. The candidates who receive the most votes in each party continue on to the general election. In the general election, the candidate who receives the most votes is elected.

Before elections, many people put signs up in their yards. Often these signs have a candidate's name on them. People put up these signs to show support for their chosen candidate. They might hope to convince others to vote for their candidate, too. But some signs don't name a candidate. Instead, they remind everyone to vote. Why might someone put up that kind of sign?

Federal, state, and local elections happen every year in Wisconsin. The offices that appear on the ballot depend on how long that office's term lasts. For example, the governor's term is four years. So, voters see candidates for governor on their ballots every four years. The offices that appear on the ballot also depend on whether it is a fall or spring election. Look carefully at the table to learn the differences between fall and spring elections in Wisconsin.

Federal, State, and Local Elections in Wisconsin

	Fall Election	Spring Election
Is it partisan?	Yes	No
When is the primary?	Varies	February
When is the general election?	November	April
Who might be elected?	**Local officials such as:** • County clerk • Sheriff **State officials such as:** • Legislators • Governor • Other executive officers, such as secretary of state **Federal officials such as:** • President of the United States • Legislators	**Local officials such as:** • Mayor • City council members • County executive • County board members • School board members **State officials such as:** • Supreme court justices • Judges • State superintendent
How often does it happen?	Every two years, in even numbered years	Every year

OFFICIAL BALLOT

FOR PARTISAN OFFICE & REFERENDUM

NOVEMBER 2, 2004

24

NOTICE TO ELECTORS: THIS BALLOT MAY BE INVALID UNLESS INITIALED BY 2 ELECTION INSPECTORS. IF CAST AS AN ABSENTEE BALLOT, THE BALLOT MUST BEAR THE INITIALS OF THE MUNICIPAL CLERK OR DEPUTY CLERK.

To vote for the candidate of your choice, complete the arrow to the RIGHT of the candidate's name. To vote for a person whose name does not appear on the ballot, write the person's name on the line provided and complete the arrow to the right of the line.

To vote on a question, complete the arrow to the RIGHT of "YES" if in favor of the question or complete the arrow to the RIGHT of "NO" if opposed to the question.

STRAIGHT PARTY

If you desire to vote a straight party ticket for all federal, legislative, state and county offices, complete the arrow to the RIGHT of the party of your choice. A straight party vote cannot be cast for Independent candidates. To vote for individual candidates of your choice, complete the arrow to the RIGHT of the name of the candidate.

DEMOCRATIC
REPUBLICAN
LIBERTARIAN
WISCONSIN GREENS
CONSTITUTION

FEDERAL

PRESIDENT & VICE-PRESIDENT
(Vote for One)

JOHN F. KERRY
JOHN EDWARDS
(Democratic)

GEORGE W. BUSH
DICK CHENEY
(Republican)

MICHAEL BADNARIK
RICHARD V. CAMPAGNA
(Libertarian)

DAVID COBB
PATRICIA La MARCHE
(Wisconsin Greens)

RALPH NADER
PETER MIGUEL CAMEJO
(The Better Life)

JAMES HARRIS
MARGARET TROWE
(Socialist Workers Party)

WALTER F. BROWN
MARY ALICE HERBERT
(Socialist Party of Wisconsin)

PRESIDENT
VICE-PRESIDENT
write-in

UNITED STATES SENATOR
(Vote for One)

RUSS FEINGOLD
(Democratic)

TIM MICHELS
(Republican)

ARIF KHAN
(Libertarian)

EUGENE A. HEM
(Independent - Third Party)

write-in

REPRESENTATIVE IN CONGRESS District 2
(Vote for One)

TAMMY BALDWIN
(Democratic)

DAVE MAGNUM
(Republican)

write-in

LEGISLATIVE & STATE

STATE SENATOR - District 26
(Vote for One)

FRED A. RISSER
(Democratic)

TONY SCHULTZ
(Wisconsin Greens)

write-in

REPRESENTATIVE TO THE ASSEMBLY District 78
(Vote for One)

MARK POCAN
(Democratic)

JAMES BLOCK
(Republican)

write-in

DISTRICT ATTORNEY
(Vote for One)

BRIAN BLANCHARD
(Democratic)

SALLY A. STIX
(Wisconsin Greens)

write-in

COUNTY

COUNTY CLERK
(Vote for One)

BOB OHLSEN
(Democratic)

BRIAN PRUKA
(Wisconsin Greens)

write-in

TREASURER
(Vote for One)

DAVID M. GAWENDA
(Democratic)

STEVE RINGWOOD
(Wisconsin Greens)

write-in

CORONER
(Vote for One)

JOHN E. STANLEY
(Democratic)

write-in

CLERK OF CIRCUIT COURT
(Vote for One)

JUDITH A. COLEMAN
(Democratic)

write-in

REGISTER OF DEEDS
(Vote for One)

JANE LICHT
(Democratic)

write-in

CITY REFERENDUM

"Shall the City of Madison be authorized to supercede the Preservation of Shoreline Parks ordinance (sec. 8.35, Madison General Ordinances), utilizing funds provided by a $2 million gift from the Goodman brothers and other sources, for the purpose of constructing a municipal swimming pool in any city of Madison park except Olin-Turville Park?"

YES
NO

OFFICIAL BA
for
PARTISAN OF
& REFEREND

NOVEMBER 2,
for

Ballot issue

(Initials of Inspectors)

Absent Elector's Ballot issued by

(Initials of Municipal Clerk or Deputy Clerk)

Certification of Elector Assistance
I certify that this ballot was marked by me for an elector who is authorized under the law to have assistance, upon request, and as directed by the elector.

Look at this ballot from 2004. Did this election take place in the spring or fall? How do you know? Which offices appear on this ballot? What else do you notice? What question were voters asked to vote *yes* or *no* on?

Presidential Elections

Presidential elections are different from elections for state and local officials. Every four years, voters in the US choose a president. Every four years, many people want to be president. Those people compete in state primary elections across the country. For example, there might be six Democrats and six Republicans running for president. During the primary, voters pick one Democrat and one Republican. Those two candidates run against each other in the general election.

Wisconsin's presidential primary is in early spring. Wisconsin voters can vote in only one party's primary.

Students hold a mock political party convention on November 2, 1968. Can you tell which candidates ran for president that year?

Voters decide which party's ballot they want. They select one candidate on the ballot they have chosen. Candidates from smaller political parties can also run for president. Still other candidates are "independent." They run for president without representing a political party. They do not need to run in the primary because they are not nominated by a political party.

After the spring primaries, each political party holds a convention. Conventions are held during the summer. Each state sends delegates to the convention. The Wisconsin presidential primary decides which candidate Wisconsin's delegates will support. In November, those presidential candidates' names, as well as state officers' names, will appear on the Wisconsin fall ballot. Fall elections are partisan. Wisconsin voters then choose both state and presidential candidates at the same time.

Why Do We Have Primary and General Elections?

Remember Robert "Fighting Bob" La Follette? He pushed for primary elections more than 100 years ago. Before La Follette's Progressive movement in the 1890s, candidates for the November elections were not chosen in a primary election. They were chosen during a convention of political party members. Only a few people were involved in selecting candidates. A powerful and wealthy group of men could select whomever they wanted.

La Follette believed he was the popular choice for governor in 1896 and 1898. But powerful men didn't want him to win. When the convention was held, they made sure that La Follette wasn't nominated.

La Follette was elected governor in 1900. He wanted to end the unfair way candidates were chosen. He felt that the citizens needed a more democratic way to choose their candidates. Many others agreed with him. In 1905, Wisconsin passed a primary election law. The law allowed the people to choose which candidate the party would nominate for the general election.

Tribal Government Elections

All Native people born in this country are US citizens. Native people can vote for their representatives in US government at the federal, state, and local levels. But Native citizens can also vote for their representatives in Tribal government. Each Native nation in Wisconsin decides:

- How many members will make up its government
- The length of each member's term
- When and how often to hold elections

For example, Bad River holds Tribal Council elections each year. Lac Courte Oreilles holds elections every two years. Forest County Potawatomi's Executive Council has six elected members. Red Cliff's Tribal Council has nine elected members.

When Tribal citizens run for office to serve their own nation, they do not run as members of a political party. But candidates must still let the people of their nation know what they want to achieve. If a Tribal citizen runs for state or federal office, they do run as members of a political party.

GETTING INVOLVED

If you're under 18 in Wisconsin, you cannot vote for federal, state, local, or Tribal leaders. You cannot yet become one of those leaders. But you may still be able to participate in elections.

In Wisconsin, people as young as 16 can volunteer as poll workers. Poll workers help people cast their votes on election day. They register voters, hand out ballots, and make sure people know how to use voting machines. They answer voters' questions and make them feel welcome. Poll workers help elections run smoothly.

"I thought it was a really good experience to know how voting works and be a part of that for my community."

– From a high school poll worker in Madison

Does your school have a student council or student government? If so, you can help make positive changes to your school community. You can run as a candidate for student council. Or you can listen carefully to the students who run and vote for the ones who have the best ideas.

In a democracy, we depend on our elected leaders to help solve problems. We expect them to act when something threatens our rights or makes life unsafe or unfair. But some problems go unnoticed until someone points them out. This is why it is so important to pay attention and take action on the issues you see in your communities, state, and nation.

We must all pay attention to our community around us. We must figure out how to fix the problems we see. Sometimes, this means finding out which elected leaders can help us make a change. Sometimes it means making change ourselves. Young people like you can get involved. You can speak up. You can take action. You can make a difference.

Pronunciation Guide

a: cat (kat), plaid (plad), half (haf), laugh (laf)

ah: father (**fah** THur), heart (hahrt), dark (dahrk), sergeant (**sahr** juhnt)

air: dairy (**dair** ee), care (kair), carry (**kair** ee), berry (**bair** ee), bury (**bair** ee), bear (bair), air (air), prayer (prair), where (whair), their (THair)

aw: all (awl), walk (wawk), taught (tawt), law (law), broad (brawd), bought (bawt)

ay: say (say), page (payj), break (brayk), aid (ayd), neighbor (**nay** bur), they (THay), vein (vayn), gauge (gayj)

e: bet (bet), says (sez), deaf (def), friend (frend), many (**men** ee), said (sed), leopard (**lep** urd)

ee: bee (bee), team (teem), fear (feer), even, (**ee** vuhn), receive (ri **ceev**), people (**pee** puhl), relieve (ri **leev**), key (kee), machine (muh **sheen**), phoenix (**fee** niks)

i: bit (bit), busy, (**biz** ee), been (bin), sieve (siv), women (**wim** uhn), build (bild), hymn (him), England (**ing** gluhnd)

I: ice (Is), lie (lI), bye (bI), aye (I), height (hIt), high (hI), eye (I), buy (bI), sky (skI)

o: odd (od), hot (hot), watch (wotch), honest (**hon** ist)

oh: bureau (**byur** oh), open (**oh** puhn), oh (oh), sew (soh), boat (boht), toe (toh), low (loh), brooch (brohch), soul (sohl), though (THoh)

oi: boil (boil), boy (boi)

oo: pool (pool), move (moov), shoe (shoo), through (throo), rule (rool), blue (bloo), fruit (froot), threw (throo), maneuver (muh **noo** vur)

or: order (**or** dur), more (mor)

ou: house (hous), bough (bou), now (nou)

u: good (gud), should (shud), full, (ful)

uh: cup (kuhp), come (cuhm), does (duhz), flood (fluhd), trouble (**truhb** uhl), motion (**mo** shun), comma (**kom** uh), magician (mah **jish** uhn), women (**wim** uhn), button (**buht** uhn)

ur: burn (burn), pearl (purl), stern (sturn), bird (burd), worker (**wurk** ur), journey (**jur** nee), myrtle (**mur** tuhl), measure (**mezh** ur)

yoo: use (yooz), cue (kyoo), you (yoo), few (fyoo), beauty (**byoo** tee), view (vyoo), feud (fyood)

b: bad (bad), rabbit (**rab** it)

ch: child (chIld), watch, (wahch), future (**fyoo** chur), question (**kwes** chuhn), righteous (**rI** chuhs)

d: dog (dawg), add (ad), billed (bild)

f: fad (fad), effort (**ef** urt), laugh (laf), phone (fohn)

g: get (get), egg (eg), ghost (gohst), guest (gest), catalogue (**kat** uh lawg)

h: hot (hot), who (hoo)

j: joy (joi), badger (**baj** ur), soldier (**sol** jur), magic (**maj** ik), exaggerate (eg **zaj** uh rayt)

k: kind, (kInd), coat (koht), back (bak), folk (fohk), account (uh **kount**), acquire (uh **kwIr**), chemist (**kem** ist)

l: like (lIk), tell (tel)

m: me (mee), common (**com** uhn), calm (kahm), climb (klIm), solemn (**sol** uhm)

n: net (net), dinner (**din** ur), knife (nIf), pneumonia (noo **moh** nyuh), gnaw (naw)

ng: long (lawng), ink (ingk), tongue (tuhng)

p: cap (kap), happy (**hap** ee)

r: run (ruhn), carry (**kair** ee), wrong (rawng), rhyme (rIm)

s: say (say), cent (sent), scent (sent), miss (mis), twice (twIs), psychology (sI **kahl** uh jee)

t: tell (tel), bottom (**bot** uhm), stepped (stept), caught (kawt), Thomas (**tom** uhs), pterodactyl (ter uh **dak** tuhl)

th: thank (thangk)

TH: that (THat), breathe (breeTH)

v: vain (vayn), of (uhv)

w: web (web), quick (kwik), choir (kwIr), what (wuht)

y: yet (yet), opinion (oh **pin** yuhn), hallelujah (hal uh **loo** yuh)

z: zero (**zir** oh), has (haz), buzz (buhz), busy (**biz** ee), scissor (**siz** ur), xylophone (**zI** luh fohn), birds (burdz)

zh: measure (**mezh** ur), azure (**azh** ur), garage (guh **razh**), division (duh **vizh** uhn)

Glossary

agencies (**ay** juhn seez): Government departments that provide services to the public

alder (**awl** dur): Someone elected to represent the people in city government

amendment (uh **mend** muhnt): A change to a law or constitution

appeal (uh **peel**): To ask that a decision made by a court of law be changed

appoint (uh **point**): To choose a person for a particular job or duty

assembly (uh **sem** blee): A house of the state legislature

ballot (**ba** luht): A secret way of voting, such as on a machine or on a slip of paper

bill (bil): Proposed law

candidates (**kan** di dayts): People running for office

cede (seed): Give up

census (**sen** suhs): An official count of everyone who lives in a certain area, such as the US

circuit (**sur** kit) court: The lowest level of trial court in the state judicial system

citizens (**sit** uh zuhnz): Members of a nation who have certain rights and responsibilities

civil (**siv** uhl): Relating to court action that has to do with private rights rather than criminal action

commission (kuh **mi** shuhn): A group of people directed to perform some duty

Congress (**kon** gris): Part of our federal government where laws are made

conservation (**kon** sur vay shuhn): The protection of natural resources like land, water, and wildlife

constitution (kon stuh **too** shuhn): A written document that contains the rights and responsibilities people have and describes how their government will work

convention (kuhn **ven** shuhn): A large gathering of people who share similar interests

debate (di **bayt**): A discussion between sides with different points of view

defendant (dif **en** duhnt): A person accused of breaking the law

delegates (**de** li guhts): People selected to represent other people at a meeting

democracy (dih **mok** ruh see): A system of government that allows the people to choose their own leaders

discrimination (dis krim uh **nay** shun): Treating some people worse than others without a fair reason

district (**di** strikt): Part of a state, city, or town that has been divided for elections

elections (i **lek** shuhnz): The process of voting to choose government leaders

enforce (in **fors**): To make sure that a rule or law is obeyed

evidence (**ev** uh dents): Information and facts that help prove something or make you believe something is true

executive (eg **zek** yoo tiv): The head of a state or local government

executive branch: The part of government that enforces laws

federal (**fed** ur uhl): A type of government where its smaller sections (such as states) are united under one central government but keep certain powers

govern (**guh** vurn): To rule, lead, or be in charge of a group of people

House of Representatives: A house of the US Congress

independent: Not controlled or ruled by another

judicial (joo **dish** uhl) branch: The part of government that settles arguments about laws and holds trials for people accused of breaking the law

jury (**jur** ee): A group of adult citizens who decide the result of a trial

legislative (**lej** uh slay tiv) **branch**: The part of government that makes laws

legislators (**lej** uh slay turz): People who make up the legislature

legislature (**lej** uh slay chur): An elected group of people who have the power to make laws for the country or state

municipal (myoo **nis** uh puhl): Having to do with a city or town and its services, such as municipal workers

nominate (**nahm** uh nayt): Suggest someone for a job, political position, or honor

office (**ah** fis): A job in government

ordinances (**or** duh nuhn siz): Laws issued by a governmental authority, such as a city

pandemic (pan **de** mik): When many people in a country or the world get the same disease at the same time

partisan (**pahr** ti zuhn): Supporting the ideas of one political party

political (puh **lit** uh kuhl): Having to do with politics, or the debates and activities among people and groups about how to govern

population (pop yuh **lay** shun): The total number of people living in a certain place

prosecutor (**pross** uh kyoo tur): A lawyer who represents the government in criminal cases

redistricting (ree **di** strikt ing): Changing the size and shape of legislative districts

represent (rep pri **zent**): To speak or act for another person

representatives (rep pri **zen** tuh tivz): Those elected to serve in the US House of Representatives or the Wisconsin State Assembly

reservations (rez ur **vay** shuhnz): Areas in the US set aside by treaty for Native nations after those nations ceded their original lands

responsibilities (ri spon suh **bil** uh teez): Duties or jobs

rural (**rur** uhl): Having to do with the countryside where not many people live

senate (**sen** uht): In the federal government, a house of Congress where the states are represented equally. In state government, a house in which districts are represented equally.

senator (**sen** uh tur): A person elected to serve in the senate

sovereign (**sahv** rin): Having the right to govern oneself and be independent of other nations

sued (**sood**): Started a legal case against someone in a court of law

suffrage (**suhf** rij): The right to vote

suffragists (**suhf** ri jists): People who led the fight for women's right to vote in the US

supreme (suh **preem**) **court**: The highest court in both the Wisconsin judicial system and the US judicial system

taxes (**taks** iz): Money paid to the government that allows the country, states, and municipalities to provide services to people

term (turm): The period of time that elected officials can serve before they must run for office again

territory (**tair** uh tor ee): A piece of land that belongs to the US but is not a state

tourism (**tur** iz uhm): Travel for pleasure

treaties (**tree** teez): Official agreements between sovereign governments

trial (**trI** uhl): The hearing and judgment of a case in court

veto (**vee** toh): To refuse to approve a bill, preventing it from becoming a law

ward (word): A division of a city

Acknowledgments

The Wisconsin Historical Society Press wishes to acknowledge the authors of the first edition of *Voices and Votes*, **Jonathan Kasparek** and **Bobbie Malone**. Their excellent work served as the foundation for this revised edition. Additional thanks to Jonathan Kasparek for reviewing this edition, lending his expertise, and sharing insightful feedback and recommendations.

Thanks also to the following colleagues who provided valuable feedback on this edition:

- **Rachel Byington**, Tribal liaison for the Wisconsin Historical Society
- **Abby Pfisterer**, director of PK–12 education for the Wisconsin Historical Society
- **Kurt Griesemer**, manager of K–12 education initiatives for the Wisconsin Historical Society
- **Tom Sheehan**, public information officer for the Wisconsin Courts System and the Wisconsin Supreme Court

Finally, many thanks to the following professionals for providing information and sharing stories for the "Getting Involved" sections of this edition:

- **Brad Lussier**, teacher at DeForest Area Middle School
- **Christina Dzwonkowski**, Camp Onji-Akiing director and Great Lakes Fish and Wildlife Commission game warden
- **Kyle Zenz**, Youth Conservation Congress coordinator
- **Marcia Gardner**, teacher at Southern Bluffs Elementary School in La Crosse
- **Rick Leib**, teacher at Oshkosh North High School
- **Tanya Schmidt**, social studies coordinator for the Oshkosh Area School District

Image Credits

Introduction

Forward statue, Maria Parrott-Ryan. Student protesters, WHi image 115506.

Chapter 1

Gaylord Nelson, WHi image 48016. US map, John Ferguson. Jim Schmitt, Scott Walker, Barack Obama, Larry Downing/Reuters/ Alamy. US map, John Ferguson. Shannon Holsey, John Hart/*Wisconsin State Journal*. Native lands maps, John Ferguson.

Chapter 2

Studying to be citizens, WHi image 112167. Mounds protest, WHi image 123836. Prairie du Chien treaty making, WHi image 3142. 1846 map, WHi image 89881, Patrick Lucey, WHi image 96394.

Chapter 3

Ezekiel Gillespie, WHi image 33364. Registering to vote, WHi image 7184. Henderson family, WHi image 4175. Suffragist parade, WHi image 5157. Lac Courte Oreilles veterans, WHi image 35070.

Chapter 4

Reservations and ceded lands map, John Ferguson. State Capitol, Photographs in the Carol M. Highsmith Archive, Library of Congress, Prints and Photographs Division. 33 Senate districts map, John Ferguson. Steineke and Stubbs, Joe Koshollek/Wisconsin State Legislature. Senate districts 12 and 22 map, John Ferguson. Governor Schrebier, WHi image 51008. Supreme Court justices, Tom Sheehan/Wisconsin Supreme Court. Native nation flags, Maria Parrott-Ryan.

Chapter 5

Jesus Salas, Obreros Unidos collection, Jesus Salas. Classroom radio, WHi image 18402. UW–Madison graduation, Bryce Richter/ University of Wisconsin-Madison. Carpentry class, WHi image 10323. DATCP workers, WI DATCP. State Parks sticker, WI DNR. Donald Driver, reproduced with permission from the Wisconsin Department of Tourism.

Chapter 6

Vel Phillips, WHi image 101443. County map, John Ferguson. County fair, WHi image 72882. Milwaukee, Photographs in the Carol M. Highsmith Archive, Library of Congress, Prints and Photographs Division. Bayfield, Dls4832 via Wikimedia Commons. Kilbourn fire department, WHi image 40708. Zippin Pippin roller coaster, Chris Rand via Wikimedia Commons.

Chapter 7

Ripon schoolhouse, WHi image 39661. Robert La Follette, WHi image 10650. Red elephant, Democratic Party (United States) via Wikimedia Commons. Blue donkey, Republican Party via Wikimedia Commons. Yard sign, Maria Parrott-Ryan. Mock convention, WHi image 7334.

Index

Please note that page numbers in ***italics*** in this index indicate illustrations.

D

E

F

G

H

I

J

L

M

V

W